MURIEL SPARK

BRYAN CHEYETTE

Northcote House
in association with the
British Council

To Susan and Jacob

© Copyright 2000 by Bryan Cheyette

First published in 2000 by Northcote House Publishers Ltd, Horndon, Tavistock,
Devon, PL19 9NQ, United Kingdom.
Tel: +44 (0) 1822 810066 Fax: +44 (0) 1822 810034.

British Library Cataloguing-in-Publication Data
A catalogue record for this book is available from the British Library

ISBN 0-7463-0907-4
Typeset by PDQ Typesetting, Newcastle-under-Lyme
Printed and bound in the United Kingdom

Contents

Acknowledgements   vi

Biographical Outline   vii

Abbreviations and References   ix

Prologue   xi

1 Life-Stories: Redeeming the Past   1

2 Half-Worlds: Writing Against Conversion   21

3 Beyond Orthodoxy: Death, Demons and   36
   Singularity

4 Transfigurations: Edinburgh, London, Jerusalem   52

5 Machine-Made Parables: From Satire to Absurdity   71

6 International Messes: Between Life and Art   84

7 Hauntings: The Return of the Repressed   101

8 Continuities and Discontinuities   118

Postscript: The Facts of Blood   126

Notes   136

Select Bibliography   142

Index   146

Acknowledgements

The author acknowledges with thanks the help and assistance of Isobel Armstrong, Gabriel Josipovici, Martin McQuillan, Laura Marcus and Nadia Valman in reading and commenting usefully on an earlier draft of this book. They have greatly improved this study. Acknowledgements are also due to the publishers of Muriel Spark's work and other copyright material.

Biographical Outline

1918   Born Muriel Sarah Camberg in Edinburgh to parents from mixed national and ethnic backgrounds.

1929–30   Educated at the Presbyterian James Gillespie's Girls' School by Miss Christina Kay who eventually inspired the character of Miss Jean Brodie.

1937   Married S. O. Spark in Southern Rhodesia (now Zimbabwe).

1938   Her son, Robin, born in Bulawayo.

1944–5   Returns to England on a troop ship after divorcing S. O. Spark who is discovered to have a violent nervous disorder. Her son is left in a convent school in South Africa until the war is over and is subsequently raised in Edinburgh by her parents. Spark finds work in the Political Intelligence Office during the war.

1947–9   Works for the Poetry Society in London and edits *The Poetry Review*.

1951   'The Seraph and the Zambesi', her first published fiction, wins the prestigious *Observer* short story prize.

1950–3   Publishes books on a range of literary figures including William Wordsworth, Mary Shelley, Emily Brontë, John Masefield.

1952   *The Fanfarlo and Other Verse* published.

1953   Joins the Anglican Church.

1954   Converts to Roman Catholicism and subsequently has a breakdown.

1957   Her first novel, *The Comforters*, published to critical acclaim.

1959   *Memento Mori* published and establishes her as an outstanding novelist.

1961   Gains international recognition and a popular reader-

	ship with the publication of her sixth novel, *The Prime of Miss Jean Brodie*.
1962–5	Lives in New York. Writes regularly for the *New Yorker*.
1965	*The Mandelbaum Gate*, set in Jerusalem, wins the James Tait Black Memorial Prize.
1966	Moves to Italy where she has subsequently lived.
1967	Awarded the Order of the British Empire.
1968–71	A period of extraordinary creativity which sees the publication of *The Public Image*, *The Driver's Seat* and *Not to Disturb*.
1978	Elected an Honorary Member of the American Academy of Arts and Letters.
1981	*Loitering with Intent* published, her sixteenth novel, and a virtuoso return to the autobiographical mode.
1984	*The Only Problem* published, which marked her preoccupation with the Book of Job and the question of evil.
1990	*Symposium*, her nineteenth novel, published.
1992	*Curriculum Vitae*, her first volume of memoirs, published.
1993	Made a Dame of the British Empire.
1994	*The Collected Stories* published.
1996	*Reality and Dreams* published. Made a Commandeur in the French Ordre des Arts et des Lettres.
1997	Awarded the David Cohen British Literature Prize for a lifetime's achievement in writing.
1999	Awarded an Honorary Doctorate at Oxford University.
2000	Her twenty-first novel, *Aiding and Abetting*, is published.

Abbreviations and References

All references to Muriel Spark's works are taken from the Penguin edition unless stated otherwise.

AA	*Aiding and Abetting* (2000)
AC	*The Abbess of Crewe* (1974)
B	*The Bachelors* (1960)
BPR	*The Ballad of Peckham Rye* (1960)
C	*The Comforters* (1957)
CS	*The Collected Stories of Muriel Spark* (1994)
CV	*Curriculum Vitae: A Volume of Autobiography* (1992)
DA	'The Desegregation of Art' (1970), *American Academy of Arts and Letters* (New York: The Blashfield Foundation, 1971)
DS	*The Driver's Seat* (1970)
FCA	*A Far Cry from Kensington* (1988)
GSM	*The Girls of Slender Means* (1963)
HER	*The Hothouse by the East River* (1973)
HF	Frank Kermode, 'The House of Fiction: Interviews with Seven Novelists', in Malcolm Bradbury (ed.), *The Novel Today: Contemporary Writers on Modern Fiction* (London: Fontana, 1977).
HIN	'How I Became a Novelist', *John O'London's Weekly* (1 December 1960)
JM	*John Masefield* (London: Peter Nevill, 1953)
LWI	*Loitering with Intent* (1981)
MC	'My Conversion', *The Twentieth Century* (Autumn 1961)
MM	*Memento Mori* (1959)
MG	*The Mandelbaum Gate* (1965)
MJS	'The Mystery of Job's Suffering', *Church of England Newspaper* (15 April 1955)

ND   *Not to Disturb* (1971)
OP   *The Only Problem* (1984)
PI   *The Public Image* (1968)
PMJB   *The Prime of Miss Jean Brodie* (1961)
R   *Robinson* (1958)
RA   'The Religion of an Agnostic: A Sacramental View of the World of Marcel Proust', *Church of England Newspaper* (27 November 1953)
RD   *Reality and Dreams* (1996)
S   *Symposium* (1990)
T   *The Takeover* (1976)
TR   *Territorial Rights* (1979)
WIR   'What Images Return', in Karl Miller (ed.), *Memoirs of a Modern Scotland* (London: Faber & Faber, 1970)
YMD   *The Young Man who Discovered the Secret of Life and Other Stories* (London: Travelman Publishing, 1999)

Prologue

Although some of her poetry and criticism is explored, this book will be primarily concerned with Muriel Spark's fiction, which includes twenty-one novels, from *The Comforters* (1957) to *Aiding and Abetting* (2000), and over thirty short stories. During a career which has spanned more than fifty years, her fictional output is rightly considered to be one of the most sustained and innovative contributions to the British novel since the war. At the same time, she has been consistently marginalized by being labelled as a 'Catholic writer'. For this reason, critical responses to her work have often focused on her as an unchanging moralist as if the issues which she addresses have remained the same. This study aims to question this approach by showing the extent to which Spark's conversion to Roman Catholicism did not, as many assume, transform her personal and literary sense of otherness. Instead, this book will focus on her playful and anarchic fiction, which disrupts the certainties of her supposedly stable identity as a 'Catholic writer'.

1

Life-Stories: Redeeming the Past

Born in 1918, Spark was nearly 40 years of age when she completed *The Comforters* (1957), her first novel. Over the next five decades, she published twenty-one novels, three volumes of short stories, and the occasional play, collection of poetry and children's work. The phenomenal success of Spark's sixth novel, *The Prime of Miss Jean Brodie* (1961) – as a stage-play, feature film and television series – has ensured that she retains a popular appeal. After gaining innumerable literary prizes and academic awards, she is now widely considered to be one of the 'most engaging, most tantalising' writers of her generation.[1] What is extraordinary about Spark's achievement is that as well as having a large international readership she manages to engage with many of the most serious intellectual issues of her time. It is typical of her work that it both gestures towards and acknowledges many of the debates and concerns of the age without, ever, being wholly reliant on them. Academic critics have begun to appropriate Spark in the name of literary and cultural theory, but this can be somewhat reductive. As Bent Nordhjem has argued, Spark's engagement with fashionable theoretical questions is always partial and fragmentary:

> Within their narrow range Muriel Spark's novels in their way incorporate all the fashionable isms of the modern scene: surrealism, existentialism, absurdism, structuralism, feminism...They do not expound them but take them as read. The Spark world is made up of what little the storm has left. The novels focus on the fragments scattered by the trends.[2]

Spark's ability to subsume the larger cultural questions of her day is in part a consequence of her formative years as a literary

1

critic. Along with a collection of poetry, her books in the early 1950s consisted of a tribute to William Wordsworth; a reassessment of Mary Shelley and selection of her letters; editions of the poems and of letters of Emily Brontë; and an account of John Masefield. Spark might well have continued as a critic and occasional poet if it were not for the publication of 'The Seraph and the Zambesi' (1951) which won the *Observer* short story prize. This story made such a profound impact that it literally transformed Spark's life. After it was published, she was immediately introduced to the editor and staff of the *Observer* and began writing occasionally for the newspaper. Because she was poverty-stricken and unwell at the time, Graham Greene offered to support her financially and was an influential patron (*CV* 192). More importantly, 'The Seraph and the Zambesi' attracted the attention of Alan Maclean, the fiction editor at Macmillan, who commissioned her to write a novel and collection of short stories which subsequently became *The Comforters* and *The Go-Away Bird and Other Stories* (1958). Such was Spark's meteoric rise as a writer of fiction.

After the mid-1950s, Spark was transformed from being a poet and critic to a much-vaunted novelist whose reputation is sustained by many of the most influential authors and critics in post-war Britain and America.[3] As a result of her late start as a novelist, Spark has been reluctant to describe herself merely as a fiction writer. In her autobiography, she states that the passage from poetry to prose felt, at the time, perfectly natural as 'the novel as an art form was essentially a variation of a poem' (*CV* 206). Her literary style, therefore, has self-consciously mixed the exactness and intensity of poetic language with the more expansive and relaxed mode of the contemporary novel. Spark, to a large extent, derived her stylistic principles from her neo-classical poetry and she has, in this regard, applied the neo-classical tenets of lucidity, precision and formal elegance to her prose. Her narrators gain their authority both from their punctiliousness and from their constant undermining of clichés and looseness of thought – most famously with regard to Miss Jean Brodie's habitual description of her girls as the '*crème de la crème*'.

In Spark's early interviews she stressed that she wished to do away with the 'wantonness' of the novel form (in stark contrast to her neo-classical poetry) and she instead intended to 'stick to a formal outline and say what I wanted to say in that limit' (HF 132). For this reason, Spark has a refined and winning literary style which deliberately masks her more discursive and extravagant intellectual ambitions. As Alan Bold has argued, Spark synthesizes the 'linguistic cunning of poetry with the seeming credibility of prose'.[4] Given the mental and physical anguish which Spark endured before she published *The Comforters*, which will be referred to below, it is clear that she did not wish to relinquish her identity as a poet as this had sustained her through some very difficult years. In characteristic fashion, she thus constructs herself as a poetic novelist or novelistic poet, the first of many such syntheses of opposites, which goes to the heart of her poised and self-confident use of language.

Her study of John Masefield, published in 1953, was an early example of a figure who combined both the poetic and narrative arts. In her preface she states that 'those parts of his life story which the poet himself has written about never fail to give the impression that life has always presented itself to him, as it were, in the narrative form' (*JM*, p. x). After *The Comforters*, Spark also began to use the art of fiction to turn her own life-story into a 'narrative form'. Patrick Parrinder has rightly dissented from the consensus that she is the most impersonal and detached of novelists and has spoken of her 'controlling personal vision; a vision which reveals itself through the . . . anaesthetisation of strongly emotive aspects of reality'.[5] In her influential discussion with Frank Kermode, Spark describes her turn to fiction from poetry, after she converted, as 'probably just a justification for the time I wasted doing something else'. She goes on to say that her novels are an attempt to 'redeem the time' (HF 132) so that her years before *The Comforters* 'won't be wasted – it won't be wasted until I'm dead' (HF 132). In these redemptive terms, her first forty years have become the waste material for much of her subsequent fiction. As late as *Loitering with Intent* (1981) and *A Far Cry from Kensington* (1988), Spark was to imaginatively reinvent her past selves and to reclaim her wilderness years for the artistic sphere.

Her memoir, *Curriculum Vitae: A Volume of Autobiography* (1992), is an account of her life leading up to the publication of *The Comforters* and covers much the same ground as her 1980s fiction. But, unlike these earlier works, it is a curiously taciturn document and tends to establish what Spark regards as purely factual links between her novels and her life-history. As a novelist, Spark does not make easy connections between fiction and reality as her writing constantly redefines the meaning and value of the stories which her characters tell about their world. But her autobiography assumes that there is a simple and unequivocal relationship between her life and work. The main reason for this single-mindedness is that she is trying to put the record straight in *Curriculum Vitae* and is countering, in particular, the dangerous 'mythomania' (*CV* 191) of Derek Stanford, a one-time friend and collaborator. As in the plot of many of her novels, most markedly *A Far Cry from Kensington*, Stanford is cast as the false story-teller who can potentially destroy an individual. As she states in the introduction to *Curriculum Vitae*, 'lies are like fleas hopping from here to there, sucking the blood of the intellect' (*CV* 11). In her autobiography, Spark remains a moralist, while in her fiction, especially after the 1970s, she is playful and ambiguous and implicates her own art in the act of lying.

Her formative experiences, recounted with considerable dispassion, indicate both the comforts and extremes that make up her early life. What is especially startling is the extent to which the book 'anaesthetizes' (to use Parrinder's term) the violence and suffering which she encountered in her first four decades. About half her autobiography deals with her comfortable upbringing in Edinburgh from her birth in 1918 to her departure to Southern Rhodesia (now Zimbabwe) in 1937. There are some euphemistic references to the 'social nervousness' (*CV* 100) in 1930s Edinburgh during the great depression and the difficulties which Spark encountered, as a young woman, in trying to obtain a job. Her subsequent disastrous marriage to Sydney Oswald Spark and brief stay with her husband in Africa from 1937 to 1944 is dealt with cautiously as Sydney's violent nervous disorders, and life-long mental instability, is alluded to with a good deal of circumspection. With typical redemptive perversity, however, Spark keeps her husband's name, as Camberg was 'comparatively flat. Spark seemed to have some ingredient of life and fun' (*CV* 132).

Curiously, Spark has restricted her experiences of Africa to a few important stories, such as 'The Seraph and the Zambesi', 'The Go-Away Bird' (1958) and 'Bang-Bang You're Dead' (1961), and to key references throughout her work. But the association between the natural beauty of Africa and a much-needed 'spiritual strength' (*CV* 128) is the beginning of a lifelong connection between art and the primitive which Spark explores in much of her fiction. In her autobiography, she speaks of the Victoria Falls as 'one of those works of nature that cannot be distinguished from a sublime work of art' (*CV* 128) and, crucially, 'there was an element of primitive truth and wisdom [in Africa] that gave me strength' (*CV* 119). The force of nature will, as we shall see, act as an important counterpoint to Spark's increasingly apocalyptic view of the decline of Western civilization.

After her return to England during the war on a troop ship, a journey which is nobly underplayed in *Curriculum Vitae*, Spark recounts the difficulties in bringing her child to London after the war which meant that he was eventually raised by her parents in Edinburgh. Many of Spark's female protagonists have young children who, rather like her view of a primitive Africa, are the receptacles for an essential set of spiritual values. In a telling story, 'The First Year of My Life' (1967), Spark presents the First World War through the eyes of a new-born child as 'babies, in their waking hours, know everything that is going on everywhere in the world' (*CS* 301). These supernatural powers of perception, a kind of innocent omniscience, are supposedly 'brainwashed out of us' (*CS* 301) after our first year. Like Spark, who also significantly came into a blood-ridden world in 1918, the baby 'had been born into a bad moment in the history of the world' and is rendered glum-looking as it witnesses 'infinite slaughter' (*CS* 303). Only after a fatuous speech by Asquith in the House of Commons, about the 'cleansing and purging' (*CS* 307) effects of the war, does the baby smile. Spark's preoccupation with suffering and rebirth in the 1950s, particularly as filtered through the book of Job, can be related to this story and eventually became the subject of her aptly named *The Only Problem* (1984).

Spark's work as a 'black propagandist' in the last year of the Second World War is represented through secondary sources in her autobiography but is dramatically rendered in *The Hothouse by the East River* (1973). After this wartime activity, where she helped to present a fictionalized version of the truth to the Germans, Spark was well aware of the effects of mythologizing the world. Her fraught time working for the Poetry Society in London, from 1947 to 1948, is recounted with relish in her memoir even though it was a clearly painful experience and is, in part, the subject of *Loitering with Intent*. Her extreme poverty and breakdown in the 1950s are touched upon in her autobiography but minimized (they are documented in detail in her personal papers). Spark wishes to avoid a too easy transformation of her suffering, by turning it seamlessly into art, which means that she often prefers silence or a more cunning means of indirectly referring to her unredeemed sense of waste. The limits of her impersonal voice can be found in her many characters on the verge of madness who constantly expose the violence and upheaval beneath her supposedly cool narrative surface. In her memoir, however, Spark has so transcended her early suffering that to reopen old wounds would, it seems, negate her subsequent success. No wonder she dots her autobiography, especially after moments of trauma, with a continuous refrain about starting 'life afresh' (*CV* 133) or a 'new life' (*CV* 211).

There is, of course, nothing unusual in a writer using his or her life-story in varied and often contradictory ways as material for their subsequent poetry and fiction. The fact that Spark, in her memoir, chooses to turn some aspects of her early life into a narrative and to ignore certain other aspects is also quite understandable. Where these issues become complicated, however, is in their being intimately bound up with her conversion to Roman Catholicism in 1954 (after a brief flirtation with the Anglican Church in 1953). Most critics have noted that Spark not only converted to the Church of Rome in 1954 but also to the art of the novel. Her acknowledged double conversion has led to the mistaken conclusion that there is an unproblematical connection between her religious and artistic quest for trans-figuration and narrative order. Peter Kemp, an otherwise perceptive and reliable reader of Spark, concludes his study with the following: 'An artistic dislike of waste, the redundant, the inaccurate, a religious striving after harmony and integration: these dictate what is in the fiction and what shape it takes'.[6] That there is, somehow, an organic coherence between her religion and art has led virtually all of Spark's critics to label her reductively a 'Catholic writer'.

The Catholic convert, in this received version of Spark, is precisely meant to close off one set of possibilities, and one version of the self, and to embrace a radically new and all-encompassing *Weltanschauung*. Spark's fiction has, as a consequence, been read as a 'spiritual autobiography' which distinguishes, above all, between the self before and after conversion. Each novel, according to this interpretation, becomes a kind of ongoing conversion, transforming the author anew, and distancing her from her previous self.[7] The abiding problem with thinking of Spark in this way is that it tends to set up an over-simple model of conversion which unproblematically splits the self into old and new, before and after, inner and outer. Conversion, in these terms, is turned into a form of determinism and becomes a rather too facile act of redemption.

The term 'convert' has an abundance of meanings and etymologies of which Spark seems to be aware. It ranges from the hardened conformities of religious conversion to a softer, more amorphous and troubling form of exchange which includes the conversion of life into art or materiality into spirituality. Even as late as her story 'Another Pair of Hands' (1985), she portrays a character who 'conversed' (*CS* 338) with herself. Spark's central figures are often doubled and redoubled, such as Dougal Douglas or Douglas Dougal in *The Ballad of Peckham Rye* (1960), and thus become their own converse. The softer form of conversion as exchange enables Spark, in her writing, to connect different realms so that her fictional domain is always perceived from competing or contradictory perspectives. What interests me about Spark is precisely the extent to which she denies a single redemptive potential within her fiction and thus disturbs a conversionist orthodoxy.

Instead of thinking of conversion as a unitary and untroubled form of exchange, Gauri Viswanathan has maintained that religious conversion is a model of 'dissent'. In her reading, conversion is primarily a form of doubleness which 'destabilizes' modern society as it 'crosses fixed boundaries between communities and identities'. According to this argument, the mixing of two different cultures inevitably creates a sense in which any one ideology can be viewed from an estranged and defamiliar-ized perspective. Far from merely superseding the past, conversion is seen primarily as an interpretative act which perceives one world through the eyes of another.[8] Spark, in these terms, reinterprets the secular novel as a parodic form of spiritual transfiguration, while her Catholicism is observed with an artist's sceptical eye. Conversion, far from being an all-encompassing orthodoxy, becomes for Viswanathan a form of heterodoxy which endlessly multiplies official discourse.

Although Viswanathan is correct to highlight the subversive potential within conversion, she overstates her case by focusing only on the question of dissent, as opposed to religious assent, even in relation to a figure as orthodox as John Henry Newman. Spark is especially enticing because she illustrates both the authoritarian and the anarchic potential within the act of conversion. Whereas most critics think of her as an unchanging moralist, I want to argue that the easy division of the self – and by extension the world – into good and evil is only one partial response to conversion. Certainly, by the time of *The Mandelbaum Gate* (1965), Spark was exploring at length the heterodox potential of her conversion, which culminated in the rejection of a moral perspective in her key 1970 essay, 'The Desegregation of Art'. By the time of *The Hothouse by the East River*, Spark was claiming that 'there isn't any war and peace any more, no good and evil...There's only one area of conflict left and that's between absurdity and intelligence' (*HER* 63).

At the beginning of her career as a novelist, in marked contrast to her later sense of amoral absurdity, Spark was to articulate the orthodox reading of conversion, influenced by Cardinal Newman, as a means of creating narrative and moral order out of the waste and disorder of her early years. Here is Spark's much-cited 1961 interview on her conversion, which she has since repudiated, where she describes Catholicism as a 'norm from which one can depart' (MC 60). She goes on to relate her reasons for conversion to her 'breakdown' at the time:

> The first reaction I had when I became a Catholic was that my mind was far too crowded with ideas, all teeming in disorder. This was part of my breakdown. The oddest, most peculiar variety of themes

and ideas of all sorts teemed in my head. I have never known such mental activity. It made me suffer a lot. But as I got better I was able to take them one at a time. ... It was like getting a new gift. (MC 60)

Catholicism, in these orthodox terms, becomes an ordering principle as well as an act of faith: 'I used to worry until I got a sense of order, a sense of proportion. At least I hope I've got it now. You need it to be either a writer or a Christian' (MC 63). Her conversion thus provided her with a renewed healthy identity and the ability to write in a controlled manner. Unlike Spark herself, critics have tended to habitually repeat these statements, as if they were writ in stone, to lend weight to her credentials as a wholly Catholic writer – in the great British tradition of Ford Madox Ford, Graham Greene and Evelyn Waugh. To be sure, while Spark was especially valued by Greene and Waugh – and *The Comforters* is not unlike Waugh's *The Ordeal of Gilbert Pinfold* (1957) – she has, above all else, mapped out her own unique perspective on the world. As she states in 'The Desegregation of Art': 'I think as an artist, I live as one' and 'the art of literature is a personal expression of ideas' (DA 21–2).

The problem with placing Spark in a tradition of Catholic writing – or any other monolithic tradition for that matter – is that she self-consciously resists such classifications. Certainly, throughout her career, Spark gained a good deal from avant-garde movements such as the French *nouveau roman* of Alain Robbe-Grillet and the British 'experimentalism' of B. S. Johnson and Christine Brooke-Rose in the 1950s and 1960s; feminist writing of the 1970s; and postmodern and magical realist fiction of the 1980s and 1990s. At the same time, she has continued the long tradition of English social realism and literary satire in much of her work and has placed these more conventional modes alongside the avant-garde. The point is that Spark only ever engages with these various literary modes in so far as they can be subsumed by her essentially singular vision. It is, perhaps, for this reason that she has not been taken up by many women critics even though her fiction, for example, might be related to the 'feminist primitivism' of Fay Weldon or the profound engagement with religion and ethics in the work of Iris Murdoch.[9] But it is clear that Spark's quirky and playful voice refuses to be contained by any one doctrine. Her abiding doubleness, above all, places a sense of history, tradition and the

9

avant-garde next to an irreverent and whimsical sense of the absurdity of all human philosophies.

Rather than categorizing her in relation to any one identity or literary culture, I want to stress that Spark's hybrid background – part English, part Scottish, part Protestant, part Jewish – has enabled her to become an essentially diasporic writer with a fluid sense of self. Always shifting in time, from the 1940s to the 1980s, her fiction encompasses Rhodesia, Edinburgh and Jerusalem and rotates, habitually, between London, New York and Rome. No one time, place or culture has been allowed to delimit Spark's imagination. Because of this, her many and varied versions of her own biography have meant that she has adamantly refused to settle on a single account of her formative years. The main problem with her designation as a 'Catholic writer', utilized by most critics of her work, is that it assumes that Spark has a stable and fixed identity and set of values which consistently informs her fiction. Ruth Whittaker, for example, in an influential study, states that all of Spark's fiction is 'written from a Roman Catholic standpoint'.[10] In contrast to this approach, I believe that Spark is constantly in dialogue with herself and, from the beginning, has played imaginatively with her own basic assumptions and the many elements which help to make up her sense of self. In short, there is always a tension between Spark's insistence on her radical singularity as an artist and her contrary insistence on the spiritual transfiguration of such differences. My argument is that her conversion to Roman Catholicism in 1954, far from resolving these contradictions, placed them in sustained dialogue.

Given the universalizing rhetoric that shapes the conventional representation of the convert, it is significant that Spark was, from the start, to continually stress her unique individuality in relation to this generalizing and categorizing orthodoxy. This is the subject of her key autobiographical story, 'Come Along, Marjorie' (1958), which is set in a Catholic retreat called Watling Abbey, a version of the Aylesford Carmelite Priory which Spark had attended. As with much of Spark's subsequent fiction, all of the characters in this story are 'recovering from nerves' (CS 163) while the narrator of the story, aptly nicknamed Gloria Deplores-you, is alienated by the conformist demands of her fellow neurotics:

As we walked along with our suitcases I made note that there was little in common between them and me except Catholicism, and then only in a mystical sense, for their religious apprehensions were different from mine. 'Different from' is the form my neurosis takes. I do like the differentiation of things, but it is apt to lead to nerve-racking pursuits. On the other hand, life led on the different-from level is always an adventure. (CS 161–2)

Her companion's neurosis, however, takes the form of 'same as': 'We are all the same, [Jennifer] would assert, infuriating me because I knew that God had made everyone unique' (CS 162). Here, in a nutshell, is the tension in Spark's conversionist orthodoxy. The impersonal and universal higher order, into which the convert is meant to assimilate, threatens to expunge her own singularity. For this reason, an unbounded individualism is at the heart of this story and much of Spark's subsequent fiction. Marjorie Pettigrew's supposedly insane refusal to conform to the norms of the retreat, and the brutal response that results from her refusal, illustrates poignantly the consequences of an authoritarian ordering principle. Instead of this conformism, Spark rewrites Gloria's Catholicism so that it can accommodate individual difference and become part of the maverick arts of the novelist. In opposition to her conventional companions, Gloria responds that: '[Jennifer] believed everyone was "the same", she didn't acknowledge the difference of things, what right had she to possess curiosity? My case was different' (CS 170). The curiosity of the artist clearly cannot exist without a strong belief in 'the difference of things', however supposedly stable and unambiguous her identity as a Catholic writer.

The 'difference of things' structures Spark's fiction in two main ways. First of all, it provides her with a range of possible national or religious identities – Scottish or English, Catholic or Jewish, European or cosmopolitan – that she plays with throughout her work. But it also allows her to differentiate within all of these categories and, at her most provisional, to deny the efficacy of all forms of classification. Spark's abiding scepticism, and refusal to settle on any one way of seeing the world, is a direct result of her 'different-from' adventurousness. Her sense of duality, of being both an insider and an outsider, feeds into her earliest poetry and short stories. For instance, in

11

'The Ballad of the Fanfarlo', first collected in *The Fanfarlo and Other Verse* (1952), Spark introduces the figure of Samuel Cramer who is taken from Baudelaire's story 'La Fanfarlo' (1848). Cramer is described, after Baudelaire, as 'the contradictory offspring of a pale German father and a brown Chilean mother', which is used as the epigraph to the poem. He is the first of Spark's uncategorizable anti-heroes and it is significant that he reappears in her seminal story 'The Seraph and the Zambesi'. In the story, Cramer has 'the look of north and south, light hair with canvas-coloured skin' but he is also, in less flattering terms, a 'half poet, half journalist' (*CS* 86). Most of Spark's subsequent protagonists or writers manqués are not dissimilar hybrid figures who, for good or ill, are firmly outside social conventions.

What is interesting about Cramer is that his hybridity is both liberating and unhealthy and illustrates Spark's fears about the confusion inherent in the 'differentiation of things'. In the story, Cramer's romanticism and doubleness result in an artistic ego which is unbounded and out of control and, because of this, he mistakes fiction for reality like many of her ensuing mythomaniacs. The point of the poem, more successfully rendered into prose, is to contrast Cramer's bogus version of reality with the real thing. In the poem, Cramer ends up in No-Man's Sanatorium, a place which signifies both his sickliness and the dangers of unbelonging. When, in the story, an actual Seraph appears in his nativity masque, Cramer, lacking a dimension outside of himself, fails to recognize it. His solipsism is the limit of his world and so he becomes unreal. As Karl Malkoff notes, Spark needs to give form to Cramer's romantic no-man's-land as 'without strict controls based outside the individual, art disintegrates, life becomes meaningless'.[11] Much of Spark's fiction is torn between the neo-classical desire to contain reality within fixed artistic forms and a romantic individualism which is essentially disorderly and defiant. In the story, she stresses a neo-classical view of art as indicated by the 'outline' of the Seraph which, in stark contrast to Cramer, 'lacked the signs of confusion and ferment which are commonly the signs of living things, and this was also the principle of its beauty' (*CS* 90).

Spark is never quite sure whether the quest for order, as in her own conversion, is not itself a form of crazed unreality as it expunges an all too human 'confusion and ferment' from the world. In another key story, 'You Should Have Seen the Mess' (1958), her deranged protagonist acts as if she can turn the messiness of life into a neatly ordered narrative. In the orthodox language of the convert, she behaves as if dislocation and displacement can be easily tidied away. While Spark's life before her conversion is essentially displaced and out of control, it is in danger of becoming reduced to a neatly ordered narrative in her fiction. It is in these authoritarian terms that Spark has been pigeonholed as one of a number of neo-classical 'Catholic novelists of detachment, like Joyce, whose god-like writer is indifferent to creation, paring his fingernails'.[12] Her often cool aesthetic surface and authorial indifference, coupled with her supposed commitment to a God-given truth, has resulted in critics stressing the sly aloofness of works such as *Memento Mori* (1959). But Spark has always been aware of the dangers of coldly expunging an uncontrollable emotional life from her fiction. At the same time as using an omniscient narrative voice, her novels also question the values of clarity and order, which is the reason why, immediately after *Memento Mori*, she published the anarchic and amoral *The Ballad of Peckham Rye*.

In her story 'Bang-Bang You're Dead' (1961), her heroine, Sybil, asks, 'am I a woman...or an intellectual monster?' (*CS* 85), to indicate the limitations of her commanding voice. Sybil's parodic childhood game, where she is constantly shot, only to 'resurrect herself' (*CS* 63), also demonstrates an enduring playfulness towards her most sacredly held beliefs. Spark's critics have tended to underestimate the extent to which her conversion not only unified a fragmented self but also enabled her to occupy more than one space in her fiction. Her faith in a universal higher authority, in other words, is thrown into disarray by a fictional practice which is plural and partial and embraces a multiple sense of self. Here the Joycean analogy is worth returning to. The Catholic authorial model, embodied in Stephen Dedalus, of the writer indifferent to creation, 'paring his fingernails', is countered in *Ulysses* (1922) by the figure of Leopold Bloom. The Greek-Jewish Bloom, in this novel, represents ambivalence *in extremis*; the impossibility of imposing meaning on the world, however much his god-like author might wish to. The ordering of reality in Spark's playful fiction is similarly provisional and always open to question. That which she wishes to transfigure invariably proves to be uncontainable and returns to haunt her.

In many of her short stories and novels, beginning with 'The Girl I Left Behind Me' (1957), characters are so radically divided that they are transformed into apparitions which haunt the page. The girl 'left behind' embraces her own dead body 'like a lover' (*CS* 360) and, in a parody of spiritual renewal, lays to rest the ghostly narrator. Her stories are preoccupied with aged or dead writers who complete their novels from the grave, or are such overwhelming spectres that they inspire others to finish their life-work. At the end of 'The House of the Famous Poet' (1967), Spark's narrator decides that the 'angels of the Resurrection will invoke the dead man' and that her worldly role as story-teller will eventually 'restore the fallen house of the famous poet' (*CS* 218). Here redemption takes both a religious and secular form and Spark was well aware of the different trajectories within these distinct kinds of exchange. Sandy Stranger, in *The Prime of Miss Jean Brodie*, is inspired to write by her conversion to Catholicism and thus enables her readers, famously, to 'transfigure' Miss Brodie. The self-transfiguration of Nicholas Farringdon in *The Girls of Slender Means* (1963), on the other hand, is the endpoint of his poetic engagement with the May of Teck Club. His posthumous sceptical scrutiny, outside the sphere of words, is of a markedly different order.

Far from being transfigured, Spark's life-story seems to return obsessively in a fictionalized form. Conversion, in these terms, is invariably ambivalent as it not only opens up the possibilities of transforming experience through writing but also exposes the limitations of such parodic mutations. Madness, singularity and unrestrained emotion are the stuff that Spark simply cannot convert into an untroubled and impersonal narrative. One of the key reasons why she is so sceptical toward the act of conversion is that she wishes, above all else, to challenge the Calvinistic belief in predestination by insisting that her personae have as open a future as possible. In her short story 'The Fortune-Teller' (1985), Spark distinguishes crucially between having a 'destiny' and a 'destination' (*CS* 335). Once her life-story is thought of as a foregone conclusion, determined by a single redemptive destiny, then other potential destinations are of necessity excluded and diminished. This determinism, which Michael André Bernstein has called 'foreshadowing', is precisely what

Spark's fictional practice works against.[13] Spark therefore not only embraces her cultural difference but also redoubles it so that it does not have a single destiny.

Spark's doubleness with regard to her Scottishness, for instance, can be seen in her telling essay 'What Images Return' (1970), which initially associates her birth place with a sense of restriction which she had to escape. In her autobiography she recalls that, as a teenager, she 'longed to leave Edinburgh and see the world' (CV 116), which was why she decided to get engaged to Sydney Oswald Spark at the age of 19 when he was about to travel to Rhodesia. This alienation from Edinburgh is reinforced in 'What Images Return', where the city of her birth has 'bred within me the conditions of exiledom', which 'has ceased to be a fate, it has become a calling' (WIR 151). Spark is explicit in the essay about defining herself in opposition to the 'Caledonian Society aspect of Edinburgh which cannot accommodate me': 'The only sons and daughters of Edinburgh with whom I can find common understanding are exiles like myself' (WIR 152). For this reason, she describes herself as 'an exile in heart and mind' and as someone who is 'moving from exile into exile' (WIR 151–2). Her feelings of exile are connected directly with her inability to assimilate into a puritanical Scottishness but also to a more creative sense of not belonging to any one nation.

At the same time as being alienated by her Scottishness, Spark in 'What Images Return' also indicates her strong attachment to the 'haughty and remote anarchism' (WIR 153) of Edinburgh, in contrast to the inclusiveness of Rome, and elsewhere regards herself as a writer of 'Scottish formation'. Appropriately enough, she thinks of her father, born in Edinburgh, as being akin to the Castle Rock or the 'great primitive black crag' (WIR 153), which belongs to the heart of the city and is also strangely incongruous. Like her father, Spark is both part of and out of place, even in her home town. Scottishness, in these primitive terms, 'has definitely had an effect on my mind, my prose style and my ways of thought'.[14] In Curriculum Vitae she especially singles out the border ballad tradition of Scottish writing which the young Muriel Camberg 'memorized . . . without my noticing': 'The steel and bite of the ballads entered my bloodstream, never to depart' (CV 98).

It is significant that Spark chooses this gothic tradition, to accompany a range of other adopted literary sub-genres – such as the desert island adventure, the urban pastoral, the school-girl's story, the ghost story, the detective novel, or the political allegory – to represent one aspect of her primitive Scottishness. In so far as the conventions of the border ballads collapse the distinction between the natural and supernatural, they chime with the gothic elements in many of her novels and are most explicitly invoked in *The Ballad of Peckham Rye*, *Territorial Rights* (1979) and *Symposium* (1990). Scottishness, in these terms, is associated with both the narrow Calvinism of Edinburgh and the gothic sensationalism of the border ballads, as well as with the sense of inevitability inherent in both traditions. But she also challenges all forms of predestination with reference to the maverick 'nevertheless principle' of her native city where a 'statement of an unmitigated fact' is invariably preceded by 'nevertheless' (WIR 153).

Spark's part-Jewishness is also redoubled and contradictory and is associated equally with the confusion and ambivalence of her unconverted self and with the radical individualism valued in her 'different-from' Catholicism. At the start of 'My Conver-sion', Spark characterizes the 'very peculiar environment' (MC 58) of her childhood which she states is 'difficult to locate': 'I am partly of Jewish origin, so my environment had a kind of Jewish tinge but without any formal instruction' (MC 58). Later on, she speaks of the 'very indefinite location' (MC 59) of her childhood as opposed to the clarity of her Catholic identity which enabled her to find 'one's own individual point of view' (MC 61). As with T. S. Eliot's *Notes Towards the Definition of Culture* (1948), which Spark had reviewed favourably, Christianity is seen as a means of imposing distinct boundaries on an excessively fluid and rootless identity.[15] Her part-Jewishness, along with her abiding sense of alienation and ill-health, was thus initially a negative principle to set against the sanity and clarity of Christian culture. In this, and especially in her neo-classical poetry of the 1950s, Spark was particularly influenced by Eliot to the extent that she was writing a book on him at the time of her conversion (*CV* 202). His overpowering presence can be found as late as *Reality and Dreams* (1996), although this novel does manage to achieve an ironic distance from him.

16

In stark contrast to her neo-classical sense of Jewishness as a negative principle, Spark is also at pains to expose the simple-mindedness of all ordering narratives in much the same way as Joyce in *Ulysses* used the uncategorizable Greek-Jewish Bloom to undermine the received language of religion and nation. It is in the context of Spark's abiding difference as a 'Gentile Jewess' that she is able to challenge, in her fiction, the redemptive promise of conversion. She, pointedly, does not describe herself as a 'Christian Jew' or 'Jewish Christian' which would have reinforced a traditional Catholic view of the transcendent power of the founders of the Church. Instead, the term 'Gentile' is deliberately open and suggests both a non-Jewish pagan and a rather prim and comic Edinburgh gentility. Throughout its composition, *The Mandelbaum Gate* was called 'The Gentile Jewesses' although, in the end, only a short story emerged with this title. Spark insists that 'The Gentile Jewesses' (1963), another tale which echoes throughout her work, is a 'nearly factual' account of her visits to her maternal grandmother in Watford (*CV* 81). She thus repeats much of this story in her autobiography. But whereas *Curriculum Vitae* tries to be 'factual' by assuming the air of non-figurative documentary realism, 'The Gentile Jewesses' is a story about telling stories and is playfully self-conscious about its claims to authenticity. Spark is acutely aware in her story of the extent to which identity needs to be performed and cannot be fixed by an outside or paternal authority.

In 'The Gentile Jewesses', Spark is able to embrace her part-Jewishness in contrast to the strictures of religious orthodoxy. After recollecting her grandmother's shop in Watford, the Sparkian story-teller comments that the 'scene is as clear as memory to me' (*CS* 308), which gives a flavour of the enticing ambiguities in the story. The clarity of Spark's memories are, after all, precisely what is open to question. Her earlier preoccupation with Marcel Proust's *À la recherche du temps perdu* (1914–22), which culminated in her essay 'The Religion of an Agnostic' (1953), meant that she was well aware of the easy claim of 'authenticity' for 'my remembrance of things past' (*CS* 300). Told from the fictionalized viewpoint of the granddaughter, the first-person narrator stresses throughout that this is just 'one telling of the story' (*CS* 308) and that her memories have been changed and modified with constant retellings. What is more, the grand-daughter often re-enacts, in retrospect, the stories told to her by her grandmother. After recalling a visit by a group of spiritualists, she 'took my grandmother's hand to show me what spiritualists did' (*CS* 311). Much of the story is performed in hindsight as if Spark is deliberately going through the stages necessary to construct a singular history. The grandmother's description of herself as a 'Gentile Jewess' is, in this way, enacted by Spark's mother and, eventually, by Spark herself. The narrative thus holds in tension the fixity of myth-making with the provisionality of story-telling.

Throughout the story, in fact, Spark's authorial voice stresses the extreme arbitrariness of her 'Gentile Jewish' identity. When told that she did not 'look like a Jew', Spark pointed to her small feet and claimed that 'all Jews have little feet' (*CS* 313). At another time, referring to her father's profession, she notes mischievously that 'all Jews were engineers' (*CS* 313). Her grandmother, on the other hand, dismissed as 'Pollacks' (*CS* 313) a group of Polish-Jewish immigrants to Watford while embracing some Londoners of German descent as honorary Jews. That Spark was to constantly play with her part-Jewish identity in her childhood can also be seen in *Curriculum Vitae*. Born Muriel Camberg, her 'foreign' name often attracted comment: 'When asked about my name I said it was a Jewish name, evidently of German origin' (*CV* 107). On her return to an Anglican convent in Bulawayo to refuse a job, because the Mother Superior was so rabidly anti-Semitic, Spark responded by saying that, 'Of course, I'm a Jew', even though, she remembers, her 'fair skin' and 'golden locks' might indicate otherwise (*CV* 134–5).

Rather than perceiving a sense of confusion that needed to be resolved, her narrative voice locates her 'Gentile Jewish' identity as a creatively disruptive force. Much to the chagrin of her grandfather, her grandmother was an active Suffragette who participated in women's marches down Watford High Street. As Spark was to illustrate at length in *Robinson* (1958) and *The Takeover* (1976), a distinctly feminine spirituality enables her heroines to challenge patriarchal authority of all kinds. Her mother's pagan ritual of bowing to the moon three times – a ritual which Spark still continues 'for fun' (*CV* 38) – is also perhaps related to the Judaic lunar calendar. By the end, her mother yokes together Christianity, Buddhism and Judaism, and this all-embracing pluralism becomes the key version of women's spirituality in the story. At the same time, 'The Gentile Jewesses' ends rather abruptly with the Spark-figure turning Catholic as 'with Roman Catholics too, it all boils down to the Almighty in the end' (*CS* 315). This limiting point of closure contrasts starkly with her childhood home where 'all the gods are served' (*CS* 315). The unresolved tension between the freedom inherent in a displaced multiple identity and the rather blunt transfiguring power of the Catholic Church was to be addressed at length in *The Mandelbaum Gate*.

'The Gentile Jewesses' is one of a number of her early stories that embrace the fluidity and disruptiveness of individual differences as opposed to the authority and sameness of more orthodox social and religious structures. At one point in this story Spark's narrator describes her grandmother as a 'white negress' (*CS* 309) and she wears, symbolically, a 'white apron' over a 'black apron' (*CS* 308), which is a binary image-pattern that is repeated in most of Spark's novels. Many of her stories set in Africa concern what she calls 'the great difficulties of mixed marriages' (*CV* 135), and 'The Black Madonna', for instance, concerns a white couple who give birth to a black baby because of a long-forgotten relative. The latter story is one of many examples of the return of the repressed in Spark's writing which, significantly given her own background, can often take a racialized form.

In a recent story, 'The Young Man who Discovered the Secret of Life' (1999), Muriel Spark's all-knowing and opinionated narrator argues that 'the lives of people hold many secrets... There was possibly no one "secret" applying to us all' (*YMD* 1–2). For Spark's storyteller, the 'secret of life' is the 'quenching' of the particular 'ghost' which had hitherto haunted her protagonist and had been 'thirsty for his soul' (*YMD* 4). Rather than a single all-explaining 'secret of life', Spark points to the 'many secrets' which make up her characters' lives and generate their own individual ghosts. The tension between a transcendent explanation of the 'secret of life' and the manifold 'secrets' of her past lives can be said to define her enigmatic artistry.

Spark is, above all, a singular paradox. Her literary influences are eclectic and quirky – ranging from Marcel Proust to Robert Louis Stevenson, T. S. Eliot to John Masefield, Mary Shelley to Max Beerbohm – which allows her intrusive authorial voice to remain unique and unmistakable. While her early fiction gestures towards a transcendent morality, much of her writing is anarchic and amoral. The constant unravelling of her most profoundly held beliefs, as embodied by her conversion to Roman Catholicism, will especially concern this study not least because her fiction, for all its superficial convictions, is constantly arguing with itself. Spark's narrative voice ranges from prim Edinburgh fact-telling to gothic sensationalism, from sublime indifference to insane monomania, but it is always witty and unexpected. She claims to be primarily a poet because the poetic mode is a means of seeing her novels as a 'whole, totally envisioned, condensed, loaded with meaning'.[16] An impersonal writer, she remains preoccupied by certain events and times in her life, and produces intensely personal but secretive works. After writing twenty-one novels, she remains as suspicious as ever of the art of fiction – whether it be social realist or gothic, satirical or experimental – but she has also genuinely extended the possibilities of the contemporary novel. Deceptively 'minor' in her use of literary sub-genres and the comic form, she is rightly regarded by many as the most gifted and innovative British novelist of her generation.

2

Half-Worlds: Writing against Conversion

At the end of *The Comforters* (1957), which was finished late in 1955, Caroline Rose goes off to write her first novel, presumably *The Comforters*. Muriel Spark acknowledged from the beginning that this work was deliberately experimental, a self-conscious examination of the nature of fictional form. As she says in her interview with Frank Kermode, it is a 'novel about writing a novel' (HF 132). In this discussion, she is quite explicit about her suspicion of the art of fiction and speaks of the novel as an 'inferior way of writing' (HF 132) when compared to the much tighter structure of poetry. The reasons for writing such a technically ambitious first work are revealed especially in *Curriculum Vitae*:

> I didn't feel like 'a novelist' and before I could square it with my literary conscience to write a novel, I had to work out a novel-writing process peculiar to myself, and moreover, perform this act within the very novel I proposed to write. I felt too, that the novel as an art form was essentially a variation of a poem. (*CV* 206)

According to this telling statement, Spark could not 'feel' like a novelist until she had witnessed herself, from the outside, performing the act of writing a novel. But, because this is a 'process peculiar to myself', Spark also needs to enact her new sense of self from the inside as well. This is why Caroline Rose is oddly a character in a novel who writes about 'Characters in a novel' (C 202). *The Comforters* is especially concerned with her sense of having a fragmented self which, if not unified, will lead to insanity. The mythomaniacal Baron Willi Stock, for instance, speaks of the 'madness of scholarly curiosity... to be interested and at the same time disinterested' (C 130). This doubleness, both inside and outside, interested and disinterested, above all characterizes Caroline's neurotically fractured self. Her hallucinations, after all, take the form of hearing voices created by a 'Typing Ghost' (C 161) which turn her life into a narrative. Writing and madness are, in this way, intimately related in this book and in much of Spark's work. For this reason, we are never quite sure in *The Comforters* of the status of Caroline's story within a story. Is she suffering from paranoid delusions (the victim of a diabolical 'plot') or groping towards a divine mystery? This sense of being on the cusp of both madness and prophecy positions her, like so many of Spark's heroines, both inside and outside her own story:

> Her sense of being written into the novel was painful. Of her constant influence on its course she remained unaware and now she was impatient for the story to come to an end, knowing the narrative would never become coherent to her until she was at last outside it, and at the same time consummately inside it. (C 181)

In the case of Baron Stock the 'madness of scholarly curiosity' takes the form of his obsession with black magic; a menacing fantasy which Caroline rejects. While Caroline needs such moral certitude to give her a sense of coherence, Spark has since learnt to enjoy such uncertainties. Her early novels are constantly on the lookout for self-deluded story-tellers, dangerous mythomaniacs and insidious poetasters in a bid to make the difference between good and bad writing a moral rather than an aesthetic consideration. But, after 'The Desegregation of Art' (1970), where she rejected this moralizing perspective, she came to realize that her own fictions may well be themselves unholy and impure. By the time of her late novel, *Reality and Dreams* (1996), she positively relished the black magic powers of her protagonist as an example of the primitive forces of nature necessary to the novelistic arts. The quest for unity, four decades after her first novel, is now seen as a betrayal of both Spark's imagination and her humanity.

The Comforters is true to the book of Job, from which the novel derives its title, as the Typing Ghost is morally ambiguous just as Job is the victim of a wager between God and the Devil. The Typing Ghost reveals that what we are reading is a fiction and that the process of imposing form upon the messiness of life is above all else an arbitrary act. In the end, the Job-like Caroline and her readers simply have to make a leap of faith so that she can end up consummately inside a God-given story. But the 'wonder' (*C* 204) of such divine omniscience, which ends *The Comforters*, is a too easy resolution of the 'disturbing authority' of the Typing Ghost.[1] Spark's later fiction was to mischievously encourage the idea of a demonic narrator who could represent, with aggressive honesty, the absurdity of contemporary life as well as the dark forces underpinning the writer's imagination.

In stressing that this novel is primarily about the transformation of herself into an artist, Spark is making explicit the unresolved tension between her conversion to Catholicism and her conversion to the art of fiction. As we have seen, there is always a conflict between aesthetic and religious types of conversion. The artistic need to be infinitely malleable and open to new and unexpected connections might be regarded as the epitome of a heterodox conversion. After all, the artist has to be constantly reinvigorated and transfigured by the act of writing. This can be seen at the point when Caroline is about to become a novelist. When she goes away to write her version of *The Comforters* she significantly leaves behind her the notes which she was making throughout. As Bernard Harrison has argued, this paradox is presumably enacted because her fiction, if it is to be an authentic engagement with the world, will be limited and impaired by her previous thoughts and preconceptions.[2] Caroline is only able to write when she leaves the novel as a 'character', because the act of creation will, if it is to be real, also transform her. Like her author, Caroline will be irrevocably changed by enacting *The Comforters* from the outside and, in this way, she is able to challenge the authority of the Typing Ghost.

Caroline Rose's experiences closely resemble those of the author in the early 1950s which allowed Spark to view her life as a narrative and thus to become her own Typing Ghost. This external perspective enabled Spark to imagine her life-story as endlessly pliable, in clear conflict with the religious view of conversion which splits the subject into old and new, before and after. Like Spark, Caroline has 'her family on the Jewish side' (*C* 38), has 'been in Africa' (*C* 48), and has something of a 'literary reputation' (*C* 67). What is more, as Alan Bold has shown, the details of Spark's therapeutic retreat in Aylesford Carmelite Priory are repeated in the novel, as is the mental breakdown which precipitated this act.[3] Just as Spark is described as 'teeming in disorder' (MC 60) before her conversion to Catholicism, Caroline's not dissimilar 'neurotic' state of mind in *The Comforters* is such that her 'brain' is 'like Guy Fawkes night, ideas cracking off in all directions' (C 36). As we have seen, Spark regards her life before her conversion as essentially displaced and out of control. By the end of the novel, Caroline is rightly perceived as an 'odd sort of Catholic, very little heart for it, all mind' (C 202), as if her thoughts alone had been placed in some kind of order.

Spark's fiction can be characterized as a whole in relation to the split between her emotions and her intellect. Caroline, in these terms, is the first of Spark's many bifurcated heroines who refuse to detach the mind from the heart or the past from the present. What is clear is that Caroline's conversion not only highlights her fissured self but also forces her to search for both an aesthetic and a religious unity. The abiding problem which she embodies is that the harmonious transformation of one's life denies the uniqueness of her identity and makes her less than human. Caroline does manage to banish the voices which haunt her, but this quiet exorcism is achieved only by her leaving her heart, in the guise of her lover Laurence Manders, behind.

As a different-from Catholic, Spark delayed her conversion for a number of years largely because she was 'put off for a long time by individual Catholics' (MC 59). In similar fashion, Caroline is oppressed by the rigid and overpowering sense of uniformity sanctioned by Catholic busybodies such as Mrs Georgina Hogg. Georgina Hogg, who runs the Pilgrim Centre of St Philomena's, castigates Caroline for engaging in a 'private Retreat' (C 30) and argues that it is 'not *Catholic*' (C 32) for Caroline to refuse to discuss the reasons for her conversion. Later on, Caroline reflects that 'Georgina's lust for converts to the Faith was terrifying, for by the Faith she meant herself' (C 147), and notes that Georgina had 'no private life whatsoever' (C 156). Georgina's Catholicism, in other words, denies the private realm and Caroline's fragile artistic consciousness. The climax of *The Comforters* enables Caroline to be 'an angel' (C 195) and to attempt to rescue Georgina from drowning. By failing to save Georgina, Caroline neatly reconciles the demands of community with her own essential inwardness. At the same time, it shows the brutality of the author in killing off a character who severely challenges Caroline's rampant individualism.

In a move that Spark will repeat throughout her career, she locates Caroline's divided character in the racial realm as if this, by definition, fixes her sense of difference. The 'half gipsy' (C 12) Louisa Jebb is especially important in this regard and is the first of a number of determinedly heterodox figures – many of whom are 'red-haired' (C 12) like Spark's Watford family – who paradoxically bring together an anarchic singularity with a transcendent sense of harmony. Louisa is the 78-year-old grandmother of Laurence Manders and is the one truly sympathetic and unifying character in the novel as the deliberately convoluted plot all seems to run through her. An exemplary figure, she is both real and surreal, introduces fantasy into the everyday, and is the model of the strongly independent woman whom Caroline wishes to become. Her 'gipsy insight' (C 116) indicates her mischievous nonconformism as well as her supernatural ability to unify disparate experiences. As one of her gang of diamond smugglers recounts:

> I understand you, Louisa. You can't bear to participate in separated worlds. You have the instinct for unity, for coordinating the inconsistent elements of experience; you have the passion for picking up the idle phenomena of life and piecing them together. That is your ideal, it used to be mine. Reality, however, refuses to accommodate the idealist. (C 22)

In her 1960 essay 'How I Became a Novelist' Spark notes that, after her conversion, she 'began to see life as a whole rather than as a series of disconnected happenings' (HIN 683). Louisa Jebb fulfils this holistic model but, significantly, in pagan as opposed to Catholic terms, as indicated by her 'alien' collection of Manders' Figs in Syrup which depict 'an oriental female... apparently worshipping a fig tree' (C 14–15). From the beginning, in fact, Spark stresses the 'instinctive' as opposed to the 'Catholic' (MC 60) nature of her imagination, and this 'pagan aesthetic' (RA 1) reached its apotheosis in her account of Marcel Proust in her 1953 essay. In this essay, subtitled 'A Sacramental View of the World of Marcel Proust', Spark sets up the redemption of Proust's pagan half-Jewishness as a momentous counter to the prevailing 'dualistic attitude to matter and spirit' (RA 1). Louisa's 'half gipsy' racial identity enables her, like Proust, to similarly harmonize 'inconsistent elements of experience' into a unified whole. Caroline especially learns from this pagan ideal with Laurence pointedly arguing that her 'coordinating mind' is able to 'piece together the mysterious facts of his grandmother's life' (C 76). Louisa was based on Spark's beloved maternal grandmother, who appears as herself in 'The Gentile Jewesses', where unity and uniqueness are similarly yoked together in the name of spiritual transcendence.

Louisa's hybrid ethnicity can be compared with Baron Stock, originally from the Belgian Congo, who is said by Caroline to have 'traces' of 'native African blood' (C 48). Unlike Louisa, who accepts her family's supernatural 'gipsy insight' (C 116), as a means of countering a rather dull social conformity, Baron Stock denies his 'concealed mixed colour', which results in him denouncing 'the blacks with ferocious bitterness' (C 48). Whereas Louisa has an 'instinct for unity', which Caroline associates with the force of nature, the all too conventional Baron Stock merely becomes naturalized as an Englishman. As Caroline puts it, 'He exhausted his capacity for conversion when he became an Englishman' (C 79). He is therefore defined by a series of superficial mindsets which isolate and disconnect him from any higher truths. As the owner of 'a bookshop in Charing Cross Road, one of those which keep themselves exclusively intellectual' (C 49), the Baron was at the centre of the rather 'neurotic' (C 62) London literary life to which Caroline had once belonged. The novel's narrator dismisses this literary circle as 'one of the half-worlds of Caroline's past, of which she had gradually taken her leave...and of which she had come to wholly disapprove' (C 48).

The fragmentation of reality in *The Comforters* includes Caroline's sense of the fundamental divisions between ostensibly similar people, such as Louisa and the Baron, and also the crucial distinction between the 'half worlds' of the past and her present search for wholeness. Her extreme aversion to Georgina Hogg's 'fanatical moral intrusiveness' (C 147) is, in these terms, displaced onto Caroline's 'Jewish side' (C 38), which is here perceived as another neurotic half-world of the past. When

Georgina recounts that she had known 'what persecution was', Caroline immediately recalls 'her family on the Jewish side with their friends, so long ago left behind her':

> She saw them again, nursing themselves in a half-circle as they indulged in their debauch of unreal suffering; 'Prejudice!' '... an outright insult!' Caroline thought, Catholics and Jews; the Chosen, infatuated with a tragic sense of themselves. They are tragic only because they are so comical. But the thought of those fireside martyrs, Jews and Catholics, revolted Caroline with their funniness. (C 38)

One of Spark's key preoccupations in 'The Desegregation of Art' is what she calls the 'victim–oppressor complex' or the 'cult of the victim' (DA 23–4) which, she believes, has an essentially segregated appeal: 'the art which condemns violence and suffering by pathetic depiction is becoming separated from the actions of our life' (DA 26). Spark associates this sense of torment with a sentimentality which isolates the individual from the world. This is reflected in Caroline's disdain for the armchair 'mock martyrs' whom she regards as 'an insult' (C 39) beside the 'real ones'. Caroline connects her own 'rapacity for suffering' (C 38) with her Jewish past and clearly wishes to transcend this Job-like condition so that it does not become unreal and insular: 'Mrs Hogg could easily become an obsession, the demon of that carnal hypocrisy which struck her mind whenever she came across a gathering of Catholics or Jews engaged in their morbid communal pleasures' (C 40). By the time of *A Far Cry from Kensington* (1988), Spark epitomized this unreal suffering in the figure of Wanda Polodok, a melancholic Polish refugee, who, like Caroline, had a 'capacity for suffering [which] verged on rapacity' (FC 7). Georgina's enforced sense of communal anguish denies the autonomy of the individual because it is used to browbeat Caroline into becoming an obedient Catholic. At the same time, a too easy transfiguration of Caroline's heartfelt fragmentation and breakdown ignores the emotional history of her own formation as an artist.

As Peter Kemp has argued, apart from Louisa Jebb all of the main characters in *The Comforters* are isolated mentally, each obsessed with their own personal reverie that is often inaccessible to the others.[4] Caroline, in needing to be different-from everyone else, is initially an in-between figure *par excellence* as she defies all categories – neither suffering nor redeemed, neither fragmented nor whole. Her fierce independence means that there is always the danger of solipsism and egomania, as there is with all writers, in the conversion of life into art. Father Jerome, the Catholic priest who successfully counsels Caroline, tries to contain her abiding sense of difference by saying 'simply [that] she was as she was' (*C* 62). This is an ironic echo, repeated in *The Mandelbaum Gate* (1965), of God's answer to Moses from the burning bush on Mount Sinai, 'I am who I am' (*MG* 28). In other words, like the unknowable Hebrew God, there is an element of mystification at the heart of Caroline's identity. Spark, in her later work, is never quite as confident in so closely associating her narrative voice with this divine authority.

Along with such theological purity, the novel introduces a range of secular mysteries from mundane detective fictions and the collection of facts, which Laurence engages in, to over-arching absences, such as the Typing Ghost, which structure the book as a whole. Most obviously, Georgina Hogg, with no private life whatsoever, literally disappears when she is by herself. Here, the contrast between her 'primitive' (*C* 147) bulk, a form of cannibalism, and the dearth of any spiritual inner life is made starkly apparent. Unlike Louisa's spiritually rich primitive instincts, Georgina's overwhelming physicality, sig- nifying her overriding materialism, merely circumscribes an absence. In attempting to embody Catholicism in person, by vampirically feeding off the emotions of its converts, she in fact betrays its basic ideals. The novel attempts to resolve Caroline's sense of disdain for 'individual Catholics' by referring didacti- cally to the 'proper obligation' (*C* 100) of Mass or the 'real form' (*C* 105) of the Christian. But, by the end, Caroline's graceful acceptance of her anonymous ghost writer is somewhat short- lived. At the point at which she is able to communicate fully with others, such as Laurence, she has to leave them so as to become a writer of fiction.

January Marlow, the heroine of *Robinson* (1958), Spark's second novel, is also closely related to Spark's own experiences in the late 1940s and mid-1950s. As with Spark at this time, January is a 'poet, critic, and general articulator of ideas' (*R* 23) who has a short-lived marriage, gives birth to a boy, and is a recent Catholic convert. She also remains completely alienated from the many 'same as' Catholics she encounters such as her brother-in-law, Ian Brodie. Her name, as well as indicating the month and town she was born in, can also be related to the Janus-faced god who could look in two different directions at the same time. Both Caroline and January are, like Janus, fundamentally divided protagonists who are split between heart and mind, constantly trying to contain the unbounded emotions of the past within a consummate but detached narrative of the present. As January states: 'If you choose the sort of life which has no conventional pattern you have to make an art of it, or it is a mess' (R 84). Caroline says much the same thing: 'For one who demands much of life, there is always a certain amount of experience to be discarded as soon as one discovers its fruitlessness' (C 35–6). Such is the fraught and often heartless relationship between the formal necessity of Spark's artistry and an uncontrollable life-story which troubles much of her writing.

From the beginning, January wishes to 'make an art' out of her experiences. Unusually written in the first person, *Robinson* starts at the point where *The Comforters* leaves off with January reading through her notebooks to see how they can be transmuted into fiction. Her journal opens the novel and gives her mind its 'bearings': 'It fetches before me the play of thought and action hidden amongst the recorded facts. Through my journal I nearly came by my death' (R 7). Like so many of Spark's later characters, January initially conforms to the conversionist orthodoxy and imagines her own death so as to transfigure the merely rational, the 'recorded facts' of her life. She is one of only three survivors from a blazing aircraft, on the way to the Azores, which landed on Robinson's island (the reclusive Robinson is its sole occupant). Writing about herself as if she had already died is, therefore, a relatively straightforward task. After all, everyone she once knew, including her son Brian, now thinks of her as 'one returned from the dead' (R 7). *Robinson*, in this way, sets up a world that is irrevocably divided and isolated not only in relation to land and water but also in terms of the living and the dead. Unlike Caroline, who discards her notebooks so as to freely engage with herself outside of any preconceived judge-ments, January retains her journal as a way of comprehending a dead self.

Spark's first two novels have, in these terms, been read as

'spiritual autobiographies' which explore the possibilities of renewing a defunct self. But this rebirth is considerably more problematical than Spark's Catholic critics imagine.[5] January, we are told, recorded her time on Robinson's island 'as if my eyes were an independent and aboriginal body, taking precautions against unknown eventualities' (R 32). Here the writer seems to be having an out-of-body experience and, like many of the ghostly figures which haunt Spark's novels and short stories, is trying painfully to unify a hopelessly fissured self. January's description of her time on the island as a 'dead women's dream' (R 36) can be read, quite literally, as a way of making fiction out of a 'dead' self. This obviously relates back to Caroline's abiding sense of being both inside and outside the narrative of her life. All of the main characters, in this regard, represent a confusion between subject and object. January Marlow, as we have seen, is both a person, a month of the year, and a place of birth. Robinson is the name of a man and also an island and, to underline this equivocation, his island's topography resembles a human body. The other two crash survivors, Jimmie Waterford and Tom Wells, also combine the location of their birth with their surnames. Not unlike *The Comforters*, all of the figures in this book are irredeemably fractured, with only January searching for a sense of unity that will not expunge her defining sense of difference.

That Robinson's island is an indeterminate space, setting opposites in play, is valued by January, who thinks of her new-found home as a 'place of the mind' (R 174) and of Robinson himself as 'near-mythical' (R 130). Her quest for harmony, however, is explicitly countered by two peculiarly orthodox Catholic theologians. Robinson turns out to be a renegade ex-Catholic who is 'constitutionally afraid of any material mani-festations of Grace' (R 99) and, for this reason, he has a strong dislike of the cult of the Virgin Mary. As with Ian Brodie, whom he resembles physically, Robinson opposes what he regards as the 'corrupt doctrine' of the Virgin Mary and has written a book on *The Dangers of Marian Doctrine* (R 78–9). The more excitable Brodie thinks of Mariology as a form of idolatry which contains 'dangerous impurities' (R 79), as it encourages the worship of a 'pagan goddess' (R 78) instead of Christ. January, however, rejects their antipathy towards the Virgin Mary as an overly masculine explanation of Catholicism and as a misguided bid to keep its theology pure, rational and male-dominated. Robinson's full name is Miles Mary Robinson and it is clear that, instead of embracing his femininity (signified by his middle name), his loathing of the Virgin Mary is, above all else, a denial of that aspect of his character. It is perhaps not a coincidence, in this regard, that Spark locates the 'sacramental' balance of 'matter and spirit' (RA 1), or masculinity and femininity, in the homosexual Marcel Proust.

Rather like Louisa Jebb, and many of Spark's subsequent heroines, January attempts to combine all of the oppositions, male and female, the material and the spiritual, body and soul, in her quest for a sense of unity. What is more, she explicitly embodies Spark's 'pagan aesthetic' and acts as one of her Proustian 'inspired pagans' (RA 1) who have historically reinvigorated the Church. She is, in particular, first characterized with reference to her grandmother from Hertfordshire who, as with the three generations of Sparkian Gentile Jewesses, pays homage to the new moon by bowing three times wherever they might be. Much to her surprise, as she is a recent convert, this part pagan ritual – which Spark still practises 'for fun' (CV 38) – preoccupies January a good deal on the Island (R 8–9, 49). But, as January herself admits, the 'pagan mind runs strong in women' (R 8) and is thus associated with the idolatrous worship of the 'pagan goddess' (R 78), the Virgin Mary. Her desire to perform this eccentric ceremony is clearly an explicit counter to Robinson's over-bearing and limited patriarchal rule. A sympathetic contemporary paganism, not unlike January's, is the subject of The Takeover (1976) and Spark's investment in such supernatural heterodoxies recurs throughout her fiction.

As with the Typing Ghost, Robinson is a false author or authority figure who wishes to determine the actions of all those under his sway. His view of Catholicism as a purely rational theology extends to his ban on the use of rosary beads along with his disdain for the Virgin Mary. January is forbidden to show his adopted son, Miguel, how to operate the beads. When January refuses to yield to the ban, Robinson steals them from her. After this incident, January remembers attending the Derby horse race 'disguised as a gipsy' and, wearing this costume, she tries to persuade Ian Brodie to cross her 'palm with silver' (R 94). Again, like the 'half gipsy' Louisa Jebb, January, as the only woman on the Island, needs to introduce the intuitive and non-rational into an essentially narrow and materialist masculine realm.

At the same time, January, like Caroline, has what she thinks of as a 'slightly masculine' (*R* 29) temperament because of her self-reliance, cool detachment and analytical mind. The reproduction of her journals throughout *Robinson* emphasizes this 'advanced' (*R* 29) side of her personality as they are full of lists, arguments and logical deductions. To be sure, the style of January's journals is a product of Robinson's frequent insistence that she 'keep to facts' (*R* 17) when writing down her observations. This is why she emphasizes from the outset her 'play of thought and action' (*R* 7) when reading these journals, as a means of bringing such dry facts to life. Such factual material can be redeemed only through a playful or spirited consciousness. In this way, the fusion of matter and spirit is at the heart of both January's theological inclusiveness and her view of the art of fiction. After Robinson disappears, presumed murdered, January takes it upon herself to judge the characters of Jimmie Waterford and Tom Wells, his two potential murderers:

> I like to take the impression of a face home with me, there to stare at and chew over in privacy, as a wild beast prefers to devour its prey in concealment ... In the course of deciphering a face, its shape, tones, lines and droops as if these were words and sentences of a message from the interior, I fix upon it a character which, though I know it to be distorted, never quite untrue, never entirely true, interests me. I am as near the mark as myth is to history, the apocrypha to the canon. (*R* 137)

Once again we have the problem of how to relate the outer and inner which for the convert, one whose past self has supposedly died, seems to be an acute preoccupation. What does the outward shape of a face tell us about the true character of an individual and its connection with their soul or 'interior'? What if this interior has changed fundamentally? Deciphering a face is rather like writing a book, according to this reasoning, never entirely true or untrue but a mixture of natural, even animalistic, intuition and a more scientific record of experience, 'its shape, tones, lines and droops'. A character is, in these terms, akin to the relationship of myth to history or the apocrypha to the canon. Fiction, for Spark, is always essentially a distortion, a true lie that arbitrarily fixes meaning. This impure fusion of reason and intuition, truth and lies, remains at the core of her art and beliefs although they become increasingly less harmonious. At the beginning of *Robinson*, January notes the way in which 'some word or thing' touches off her memory and is 'almost sacramental' (*R* 8). Christian sacrament and artistic creation are therefore seen, at this early stage, to spring didactically from the same ideal union. After the 1970s, however, Spark will focus increasingly on the unruly spontaneous and bestial side (devouring its prey) of her novelistic arts.

As many critics have noted, the setting of her second novel on an island has obvious links to Daniel Defoe's *Robinson Crusoe*, *The Swiss Family Robinson* and William Golding's *Lord of the Flies*. In fact, the date of the air crash, 20 May 1954, coincides with the year of publication of Golding's novel. But, unlike these earlier works, Spark insists throughout *Robinson* that her island is essentially mythical and boundless and not merely a means of isolating the individual from society. In an implied reference to Golding's *Pincher Martin*, there is even a strong suggestion that January has dreamt her whole experience and that the island might be 'apocryphal', a 'trick of the mind' (*R* 174–5). Such thoughts transform her journal from a factual account into something else entirely, 'a sea-change so that the island resembles a locality of childhood, both dangerous and lyrical' where 'all things are possible' (*R* 175). The island is a perfect objective correlative for her need to fuse opposites as it is both an individual and a place, real and unreal.[6] Paradoxically, the very indeterminacy of this locale enables January to resolve her sense of a split self. For this reason, January notes that 'Looking forward to going home, I necessarily looked backward' (*R* 91). When Jimmie Waterford echoes John Donne's well known sentiment that 'no man is an island', January disagrees, 'some are ... their only ground of meeting is concealed under the sea' (*R* 22). Here, in purely aesthetic terms, is the sacramental mixture of matter and spirit (or land and water) which January strives for.

At one point in the novel, January notes significantly that the three survivors from the air crash were 'on the same island but in different worlds' (*R* 144). Both Jimmie Waterford and Tom Wells, when compared to January, are monodimensional figures, 'two different types of the melodramatic mind; one coloured by romance, the other by crime' (*R* 144). Tom Wells, not unlike Baron Stock, is a promoter of the occult and, along with Georgina Hogg, is the first of Spark's many professional blackmailers, who appear in virtually all of her novels. Spark seems to regard the blackmailer as the segregator *par excellence* who forces others to split and divide their lives into public and private realms. The romantic Jimmie Waterford has a strong element of 'rootless European frivolity' (*R* 93) about him and, as with Samuel Cramer, mythologizes the world according to his private fantasies. Both figures, that is, have unbounded egos and create false and dangerous myths about themselves and those around them. If Robinson cannot see beyond the merely factual, then Jimmie and Tom are completely detached from actuality. All three are examples of masculine excess, of splitting the world into matter and spirit, in stark contrast to January's rather programmatic sense of unification.

January is at pains to associate her feminine playfulness with that which goes beyond the merely rational. To this extent there is an important link between her identity as a woman and a wider vision of social morality. Because the cult of the Virgin Mary is regarded by Brodie and Robinson as a dangerous impurity, January sees it as her role to introduce even more impurities into such a narrow and bigoted worldview. The misguided pursuit of purity, echoing *The Comforters*, is challenged by the insistence on the essential difference of things. Ian Brodie's misogyny also includes a rampant homophobia where homosexuality is described as 'disgusting and unnatural' (*R* 96–7). He is, in other words, an extreme example of a same-as Catholic as he acts 'as if the whole world consisted of the class of society with which [he was] familiar' (*R* 97). In the end, January rejects Robinson's extreme form of seclusion because there is 'no such thing as a private morality' (*R* 161). His refusal to accept the three survivors on his island, in the name of his systematic isolation, goes to the heart of her disagreement with him. Robinson complains that his 'regulated' (*R* 162) life was disrupted by the plane crash. January's rejoinder is crucial: 'any system … which doesn't allow for the unexpected and the unwelcome is a rotten one' (*R* 162). Spark's ability to accommodate the 'unexpected and the unwelcome' will give an anarchic edge to her subsequent fiction.

The publication of *Robinson* marked the end of Spark's apprenticeship as a novelist and also of her initial phase of autobiographical fiction. Her first two works span the history of the novel in general and show the extent to which Spark is searching for a suitable fictional form to recreate her own experiences. *Robinson* goes back to the epistolary roots of the novel, in its widespread use of journals as well as its association with Daniel Defoe, and *The Comforters* is self-consciously in the tradition of avant garde modernism. Both works are preoccupied with the identity of their heroines and their formation as suffering artists. In rejecting Robinson's 'private morality' Spark is declaring her enduring unease with the novel form in general which, after all, creates an individual world with its own internal logic and ethical system. Her next three novels, published in quick succession between 1959 and 1960, move away from an explicitly autobiographical mode and begin to explore some of the unresolved tensions in *The Comforters* and *Robinson*. By acknowledging a transcendent morality, beyond her singular fictions, Spark of necessity rejects the impure desires that are the very life-blood of her writing. The struggle to incorporate the 'unexpected and unwelcome' (*R* 162) into an impersonal God-given morality will especially preoccupy her in her next three books.

3

Beyond Orthodoxy: Death, Demons and Singularity

In a reversal that will continue throughout her career, Muriel Spark's next three novels veer sharply away from the autobio-graphical mode of her first two works. The first-person narrator in *Robinson* is now replaced by a disembodied voice which is literally and figuratively detached from what is going on. As we shall see, each of Spark's books is in dialogue with the others and each zigzags between an unruly past and an indifferent present-day narrator. After initially descending into the world of unrestrained emotions and unconverted history, she now finds refuge behind an impersonal and god-like narrator. Her neo-classical third novel, *Memento Mori* (1959), could not be further from her life-stories and has come to represent Spark at her most didactic and orthodox. More tightly structured than her first two books, Spark's omniscient story-teller has become cooler, more confident, and removed from the chaos that it recounts. Her fictional universe has also grown smaller, more limited, and gives the illusion of providing a neat slice of life which the reader can easily assimilate. At the same time, Spark disrupts a facile realism by making her work openly fictive so that it can only be judged in its own literary terms. She explains her method as follows:

> When I become interested in a subject, say old age, then the world is peopled for me – just peopled with them. And it is a narrow little small world, but it is full of old people, full of whatever I'm studying. They're the centre of the world, and everyone else is on the periphery. It's an obsession until I've finished writing about them. (HF 133)

Memento Mori is, in this fashion, populated almost exclusively with characters over the age of 70. This enables her to create a world that is both self-consciously artificial, in which she can easily insert the supernatural, and yet which also has the ring of truth. As with all of her books, Spark thoroughly researched *Memento Mori* and spent some time visiting a geriatric ward in a hospital. She dedicates the novel to Teresa Walshe, a Staff Nurse who helped her in this task. In *Curriculum Vitae* Spark remembers at the age of 11 'minding and watching' (*CV* 91) her maternal grandmother after she had suffered a stroke. This awareness of old age, she believes, formed a starting point for *Memento Mori*. After Spark's grandfather had died in Watford, her cherished grandmother moved up to the Edinburgh family home when Spark was only 8 years old. The contrast between the grandmother's extraordinary spirit, recounted in 'The Gentile Jewesses', and her physical decline is a painful and lasting one. As well as the need for a more controlled and more compressed form, the subject matter of old age relates especially to the split between matter and spirit or body and soul, which continues to preoccupy Spark. In her 1960 essay on 'How I Became a Novelist', she explains the theme of her third novel in relation to these concerns as well as its literary form. Recalling her trips to Edinburgh to see friends and relatives of her mother when they were dying in hospital, she remembers being

> impressed by the power and the persistence of the human spirit. They were paralysed or crippled in body, yet were still exerting characteristic influences on those around them and in the world outside. I saw a tragic side to this situation and a comic side as well. (HIN 683)

Although *Memento Mori* concerns itself with the theme of mortality, it is determinedly not a morbid novel. Focusing exclusively on old age means that the fissure between mind and body can now be examined *in extremis* with both comic and tragic results. The different possible responses to this split are highlighted in the novel's various epigrams which open the book. They range from Yeats's fury at his body's decline, to the divine veneration of the elderly, to the absolute need to remember the Four Last Things, 'Death, Judgement, Hell and Heaven' (*MM* 5). In a masterful stroke, of great economy and concision, Spark introduces the surreal figure of Death in the guise of an unwelcome and unexpected telephone caller who opens the novel and who then subsequently rings every other major character. Assuming different voices, depending on who is being addressed, the mysterious caller tells each recipient an essential truth, 'Remember you must die'. This phrase is, after all, the literal translation of the eponymous 'Memento Mori' and acts something like a Greek Chorus, taking Spark's characters beyond the physical realm. On hearing this truth each person reacts in a different way, related to the spiritual health of the receiver, which varies from those who find it merely a threat, to those who find it a reassurance, to those who simply deny that they are reaching the end of their lives. Spark has been described, as a 'reactionary allegorist' although she still has a characteristic lightness of touch even in *Memento Mori*.[1]

In *Robinson* the death of the author enables January Marlow to achieve a momentary sense of redemption and spiritual unification to counter her hopelessly fissured identity. By contrast, the avoidance of death-in-life is illustrated by Percy Mannering, the 80-year-old poetaster in *Memento Mori*, 'who did not acknowledge the idea of revival...since he did not recognize the interim death' (*MM* 97). At one point, Percy is significantly described as 'half-beast, half-man, instead of half-poet, half-man' (*MM* 22). January, we remember, also combines the bestial with the rational and it is her ability to balance these two opposing forces that gives her a sacramental view of life. Percy, on the other hand, with his unbounded artistic ego, is completely certain of his opinions and remains obsessed with his petty literary disputes throughout the novel. Like Samuel Cramer and Baron Stock before him, he is an unruly hybrid figure who confuses his own personal manias with reality. Without a belief in the ever-presence of death or suffering, a motif throughout all of Spark's fiction, life becomes anaemic and is reduced, in the case of Percy, to rather puerile man-made concerns.

Although perhaps an equally theological novel, *Memento Mori* lacks the self-congratulatory tone which sometimes creeps into *Robinson*. This is because instead of locating its truths in a single voice, with which the reader is encouraged to identify, Spark gives three different characters various insights into the mysterious telephone caller and the meaning of the resonant phrase, 'Remember you must die'. The first of these is Henry Mortimer, a retired Chief Inspector who is called upon to investigate the matter. Unsurprisingly, given his blanket endorsement by the Sparkian narrator, the 'power of unity... exists' in his 'face' (*MM* 140) and he is able to immediately grasp that the 'offender is Death itself' (*MM* 142). As his surname *Mort*imer suggests, the former CID man understands the true import of the so-called 'Hoax-Caller' (*MM* 141):

> If I had my life over again I should form the habit of nightly composing myself to thoughts of death. I would practise, as it were, the remembrance of death. There is no other practice which so intensifies life. Death, when it approaches, ought not to take one by surprise. It should be part of the full expectancy of life. Without an ever-present sense of death life is insipid. You might as well live on the whites of eggs. (*MM* 150)

In a set-piece scene, which parodies formulaic detective fiction, those who regard themselves as victims of a Hoax Caller (as the newspapers would have it) descend on Henry so that he can solve the mystery of their supposed maltreatment. Spark constantly incorporates literary clichés into her novels in a redemptive bid to breathe new life into them. Henry's metaphysical response to what others take to be a purely rational issue, a mundane and solvable question of identity, is a good example of this renewal of empty 'scenarios' (as she calls them). Not unlike G. K. Chesterton's Father Brown, Henry states that 'The trouble with these people...is they think the C.I.D. are God, understanding all mysteries and all knowledge. Whereas we are only policemen' (*MM* 153). A good many of Spark's books are constructed around the death of a central character as a means of highlighting the 'insipid' nature of a world without pain. Ever since her essay on 'The Mystery of Job's Suffering' (1955), Spark has been struggling with the necessity of death and suffering in both her life and work. She eventually returns to this conundrum, in much less didactic terms than *Memento Mori*, in *The Only Problem* (1984).

While Henry grasps, in the abstract, that death is 'part of the full expectancy of life', he significantly does not do so from an orthodox Catholic perspective. Part of the strength of this book, which indicates Spark's ingrained resistance to dogmatism, is that she allows three profound but radically opposed responses to the remembrance of death. Not unlike January, Henry offers a pagan interpretation of this question as illustrated by his many grandchildren, whom he is seen playing with, which indicates the generations in harmony. Like all of Spark's subsequent 'inspired pagans' (*RA* 1), Henry, through his all-important summer yachting, is seen to combine the natural world with the life of the mind. By seeing death as part of the life-cycle, as something which intensifies life, he manages to redeem it from its 'terrifying absurdity' in Peter Kemp's felicitous phrase. For Henry and his beloved wife (a happy marriage is itself unusual in Spark's work), 'age and death are simply part of an inevitable natural process'.[2] It is not a coincidence, with regard to the feminized natural realm, that Henry's caller is 'always a woman, gentle-spoken and respectful' (*MM* 153).

Later on in the novel, Jean Taylor, one of Spark's 'nearly masculine' (*MM* 70) idealized Catholic converts, repeats Henry's words almost verbatim: 'the author of the anonymous telephone calls is Death himself' (*MM* 175). But she goes on, 'If you don't remember Death, Death reminds you to do so. And if you can't cope with the facts the next best thing is to go away for a holiday' (*MM* 175). The comic archness of this bathetic statement, as well as the necessity of coping with momentous facts, clearly has Spark's authorial approval. But while Jean Taylor locates death and her own physical suffering in the supernatural realm, as the first of the Four Last Things, Henry Mortimer sees it as an essential part of the life-force of nature. As we have seen in *Robinson*, Spark, from the beginning, wished to include a different-from 'pagan aesthetic' (*RA* 1) within her Catholic theology. These associations between paganism, womanhood and the origins of the Church were to reach their apotheosis in *The Takeover* (1976). But Spark's later heterodoxy is implicit even in her most orthodox works.

Unusually for Spark, who is often suspicious of her literary doppelgängers, the third character to have a spiritual insight into the book's leitmotif is a novelist herself. A maverick Catholic, Charmian Colston, aged 86, is a once famous author whose work is being revived. She has some of Spark's life-story, including a breakdown in her youth, and much of her scepticism towards the art of fiction. But the renewed interest in Charmian's work helps to physically rejuvenate her, which illustrates, a little too obviously, the restorative unity of the life of the body and that of the mind. She has had a stroke and is 'muddled about most things' but the one thing that she is 'quite clear on' is 'the subject of her books' (*MM* 16). Later on we are told that 'her novelist's mind by sheer habit still gave... disjointed happenings a shape' (*MM* 57) and that 'her mind works associatively' (*MM* 60). Her ability to order the world internally enables her to gain the necessary perspective so that she, too, can go beyond its mundane realities.

In a key exchange with Guy Leet, she defines the art of fiction as being 'very like the practice of deception' (*MM* 187). But when he asks her whether 'the practice of deception in life [is] an art too?' her answer is significant: 'In life... everything is different. Everything is in the Providence of God' (*MM* 188). Where Charmian differs from many of her fellow novelists is that she realizes, like her creator, that her writing is nothing more than a deception and that there is a radically different way of perceiving the world. Instead of responding to the message on the telephone as a threat, as her appropriately named husband Godfrey (God-free) does, she states simply that one should 'treat it as it deserves to be treated... Neither more nor less' (*MM* 124). She later tells a newspaper reporter that even though her memory is failing her she does not 'forget my death, whenever that will be' (*MM* 127).

What brings Henry Mortimer, Jean Taylor and Charmian Colston together is that they are all able to unify matter and spirit, or the natural and the supernatural, albeit from three incongruous and partial perspectives. Taken as a whole they represent a diverse way of understanding the eternal verities although, it might be argued, each of their individual perspectives – pagan, orthodox Catholic, aesthetic – is by itself limited. In contrast with this troika, however, virtually every other character in the novel is a hollow figure. That is, they are all driven by purely animalistic desires or what has been accurately described as 'husks of appetite'.[3] Whether it be Godfrey Colston's lust, Percy Mannering's egomania, Lisa Brooke's vanity, Lettie Colston's bullying, or Alec Warner's fanatical rationalism, all of these figures occupy the purely physical realm. They are, in other words, split off from their inner selves and divorced from reality. The 'mass hysteria' (*MM* 152) which is claimed to explain the mysterious telephone caller is merely a way of avoiding the truth. In denying their own mortality each has to rely on their own terribly flawed personal obsessions. Lettie Colston's paranoid fantasy that a criminal gang is out to get her proves, inevitably, to be a self-fulfilling prophecy. Such unreal myths, as always, can be lethal.

Memento Mori is brutally secure in its moral certainties in so far as its characters occupy either a visionary spiritual plain or a mundane materialist sphere. Alec Warner, like Laurence Manders and Miles Mary Robinson before him, is fascinated by fact-finding, which places him in a long line of narrow masculine rationalists who are dotted throughout Spark's corpus. His conversations with Jean Taylor can be seen as crystallizing the clash of values in the novel and creates a chasm between them. When he asks her whether 'other people are real' (*MM* 70), there is a plausible sense in which 'other people' in the novel fundamentally do not exist. Like Georgina Hogg before them, most of Spark's benighted characters are located only in the physical realm and are therefore, in both life and art, monodimensional. Jean responds by saying that the 'graveyard is a kind of evidence ... that other people exist' (*MM* 70) and, to a large extent, *Memento Mori* brings to life this graveyard as most of the book's dramatis personae eventually occupy it. As Jean makes clear, 'Being over seventy is like being engaged in a war. All our friends are going or gone and we survive amongst the dead and the dying on the battlefield' (*MM* 37). What gives this novel its beguiling energy, in contrast to its moralizing theme, is precisely the sense of each character fighting for his or her life.

For much of the novel, Jean is based in the geriatric Maud Long Medical Ward with twelve other derogatorily named 'grannies'. None of them is capable of much movement and, for this reason, they manifest perfectly the life of the spirit. This is the ideal counterpoint to the meaningless materialism, embodied in Alec Warner's card index and Lettie Colston's endless rewriting of her will, of those outside the hospital. At the apex of the material world is a figure of absolute evil, Mrs Pettigrew, who attempts to blackmail Godfrey Colston and whose brutishness links much of the plot together. In *Robinson*, Curly Lonsdale contended that 'life is based on blackmail' (*R* 137) and, like all of Spark's ubiquitous extortionists, Mrs Pettigrew specializes in dividing reality into the private and public sphere, turning knowledge into power and thereby making it fractured and unreal. Because so many of Spark's characters are split off from themselves, they inevitably have secrets to hide and are prey to blackmailers. In eventually acknowledging her characters' 'many secrets' (*YMD* 1), Spark's later works are able to engage openly with the dark forces that have made them. While the god-like narrator and the evil Mrs Pettigrew could not be further apart, such depraved figures and her fictionalized story-tellers will eventually be brought much closer together.[4]

Memento Mori extends Spark's preoccupation with a split self by creating a fictive world where virtually everyone is deeply fissured. The disruptive voice on the telephone, not unlike the Typing Ghost in relation to Caroline, reminds each character to engage with the life of the spirit so as to have a more complete sense of reality. But only Spark's holy trinity – Henry Mortimer, Jean Taylor and Charmian Colston – achieve this end, and even this select group merely offers a series of individual and incompatible truths. The majority of Spark's dramatis personae live out a lie as they believe that they can somehow avoid the presence of their own mortality. Some, such as Mrs Pettigrew and Alec Warner, thrive in these profoundly unpleasant circumstances. But *Memento Mori* is a disturbing novel because its macabre subject matter is combined with an all-pervading sense of madness. In this ruptured universe, knowledge of the metaphysical realm is presented as a form of sanity and those who live exclusively in the physical domain are driven insane by their petty obsessions. The voice at the end of the telephone is not a lunatic, as most of her infuriated characters imagine, but the absolute truth. Only those who cannot see beyond themselves are, in effect, deranged. In this oddly brutal world, one can only be redeemed by going beyond the messiness of life. Spark's solipsists and obsessives are, by definition, doomed to oblivion precisely because they are unable to transcend the limits of the self.

Spark in *Memento Mori* is at her most pessimistic as she has plainly given up on the idea of individual agency and the autonomy of her characters. Having said that, *The Ballad of Peckham Rye* (1960), based partly on her time living in south London, deliberately counters this despairing stance and focuses especially on the singularity of the novelist's voice. If the individual is condemned to self-negation, when seen in the light of eternity, where does this leave the distinct role of the writer? In stark contrast to what has gone before, Spark's droll fourth novel is described by her as 'light and lyrical – as near a poem as a novel could get' (HIN 638). Her next book is deliberately written in reaction to the complexity and range of *Memento Mori* and employs a simpler form and a purer mode of storytelling. In a considerably more hopeful tenor, it introduces the first of her amoral novelists manqués, both good and evil, attractive and repulsive, who help her to explore the difficulties of retaining a singular perspective in the light of the God-given certainties of existence.

Most critics have mistakenly regarded Dougal Douglas, the mischievous trickster at the heart of *The Ballad of Peckham Rye*, as a wholly diabolical figure. While the red-haired Dougal is obviously a figure out of Scottish mythology, especially the border ballad tradition, he is also a notably appealing character. The redness of his hair has often been said to indicate Dougal's diabolical nature but it can also be related to the 'reddish hair' (*CV* 107) of Spark herself. In these terms, he is precisely a different-from writer manqué who, in the most heterodox and anarchic terms, wishes to bring together the natural and supernatural realms. Although he is engaged in 'human research' (*BPR* 18), rather like Laurence Manders and Alec Warner before him, he is not an empty fact-finder who believes that he can reduce human nature to the level of a card index. Instead, he aims to 'discover the spiritual well-being' (*BPR* 17) of Peckham Rye and he is thus asked by Mr Druce, the manager of Meadows, Meade & Grindley, to 'bring vision into the lives of the workers' (*BPR* 16). As he later tells Druce, 'vision... is the first requisite of sanity' (*BPR* 64) which is, in short, a summary of the plot of *Memento Mori*. Douglas, in other words, is another of Spark's spiritual catalysts, not unlike the Typing Ghost or the anonymous voice on the telephone, who bring together sacramentally the inner and outer realms of less visionary individuals.

The reason why Douglas is so often misread as utterly devilish is that he playfully represents himself in these terms. He claims to have had an operation to remove 'two horns' (*BPR* 77) on his head and his 'deformed shoulder' (*BPR* 17) also, of necessity, conjures up associations with historical figures of evil such as Shakespeare's Richard the Third. He tells Humphrey Place that, 'I'm supposed to be one of the wicked spirits that wander through the world for the ruin of souls' (*BPR* 77). But rather than claiming to be a 'wicked spirit' as such, Douglas is commenting with subtlety on what he is 'supposed to be' or how others perceive him. Even when he encourages these perceptions he is still not straightforwardly on the side of wickedness. After asking Merle Coverdale whether she is a 'free woman or a slave' (*BPR* 30), which helps her to question her barren existence, he decides to 'pose like an angel on a grave' (*BPR* 30) in a local cemetery. Once again, Douglas self-consciously performs the role of an 'angel-devil' (itself an ambiguous designation) rather than actually claiming to be the devil itself: 'He posed like an angel-devil, with his hump shoulder and gleaming smile, and his fingers of each hand widespread against the sky' (*BPR* 30).

As the name Dougal Douglas suggests, especially as it is reversed halfway through the work, everything to do with him is doubled and redoubled rather than located entirely on one side of the moral spectrum. He is, as he often tells us, 'crooked by nature' (*BPR* 15) and so he is never quite what he seems. From the beginning, he is able to 'change...his shape' (*BPR* 16) and assume other guises, which, to be sure, links him with traditional Scottish versions of satanic figures such as the protagonist of James Hogg's *The Private Memoirs and Confessions of a Justified Sinner* (1824) or Robert Louis Stevenson's *The Strange Tale of Dr Jekyll and Mr Hyde* (1886). But the doubleness and crookedness of Douglas, making him impossible to pin down, also undermine the idea of him as a figure of pure evil. As Karl Malkoff rightly argues, much of what Douglas does is good, as he offers those around him 'freedom from the confines of artificial moralities'.[5] After all, the residents of Peckham are explicitly presented as shallow and mechanical and in dire need of the spiritual substance which Douglas provides.

The Ballad of Peckham Rye is, as many have noted, reminiscent of the Scottish border ballads in the simplicity of its mytho- logical story-line, its supernatural undertones, and the Scottish- ness of its central figure. After all, the first chapter of the book makes clear that the 'affair' (*BPR* 14) of Humphrey Place leaving his bride at the altar is now 'a legend' (*BPR* 14) and can be recounted in a variety of distinct ways. What is more, the current version of this affair is, in all likelihood, that told by Douglas himself. This is because Douglas throughout the book is writing the autobiography of Maria Cheeseman and, much against her desires, he insists on adding a number of fictional chapters concerning his time in Peckham. Later on, in *Loitering with Intent* (1981), Spark's heroine Fleur Talbot will also fictionalize her client's memoirs when she works for the Autobiographical Association. Like Fleur, Douglas's playful deceptions define him as having a novelist's 'crooked' (*BPR* 76) mentality, which is why, in the end, he becomes the real thing: 'he gathered together the scrap ends of his profligate experience – for he was a frugal man at heart – and turned them into a lot of cockeyed books, and went far in the world' (*BPR* 142). One of the highest virtues for Spark is that of frugality or economy (a favourite word of hers) precisely because these terms, according to the conversionist orthodoxy, indicate the control of waste.

Douglas is continually described, by virtually everyone he meets, as being 'different' (*BPR* 25) and his different-from vision of 'another world than this' (*BPR* 143) is absolutely paramount. Like much of her later work, *The Ballad of Peckham Rye* is an impure mixture of social realism and surreal mythology. On the one hand, it mimics so-called working-class novels of the time and is full of wry details about street-fighting, pub culture and popular dancing of the 1950s. At the same time, it echoes her earlier use of traditional forms of story-telling such as 'The Ballad of the Fanfarlo' (1952), and it has to be said that in these terms one learns very little about the social realities of Peckham. Here Douglas's defining peculiarity, his anarchic presence, is reflected in Spark's hybrid literary concoction. Whereas the spiritual realm in *Memento Mori* is universalized and flattens out individual difference, Douglas, who causes mayhem wherever he goes, is above all determined by his radical singularity. His singular refusal to conform to the moribund social norms of

Peckham (or anywhere else for that matter) ultimately points to his prophetic status. It may be that Douglas's facile ability to change shape is a type of 'fraudulent conversion' (*B* 9, 109, 189), a phrase dotted throughout Spark's next book. But even such limited kinds of transformations, typified by the novelist's art, are shown to be a salutary response to the mechanical, changeless lives of the people of Peckham.

In *The Bachelors* (1960), published in the same year as *The Ballad of Peckham Rye*, Spark presents her novelist manqué in more rounded and moderate terms which, in the end, makes this work seem overly didactic and heavy-handed. Rather like *Robinson*, whose setting is wholly mythological, the London of this novel is more a 'place of the mind' (*R* 174) than an actual metropolitan city. Whereas Douglas plays at being a devil-figure and becomes a writer, Ronald Bridges is 'possessed by a demon' (*B* 14), that is he is an epileptic, but only thinks like an author. Spark, in this work, is exploring the extent to which the novelist's imagination and god-like pretensions are, in the end, depraved. A belief in original sin, as is affirmed in *The Bachelors*, means 'that all the utterances of man are inevitably deep in error' (*B* 126). Because Douglas is the epitome of unreliability and crookedness, and gains worldly success, he can only ever be viewed through a traditional demonizing mindset. Seeing Douglas as the devil, however, lets every other character off the hook, just as dismissing the anonymous telephone caller as a lunatic in *Memento Mori* avoids the need for any introspection. But Spark in *The Ballad of Peckham Rye* does seem to have an emotional commitment to the extravagance and anarchism of her mischievous protagonist that is missing from either *Memento Mori* or *The Bachelors*. In these latter works, Spark restrains her feelings for the sake of a cooler, more aloof account of the individual in relation to a set of values which lie beyond the self.

Ronald Bridges is a much less extreme figure than Douglas, as he is situated neither in the natural nor in the supernatural realm but is instead a bridge, as his name suggests, between these two spheres. His epilepsy combines the madness or 'obsession' (HF 133) of the writer with the abiding necessity, first noted in *The Comforters*, to see oneself from the outside. He argues that during an epileptic seizure he has the conscious sense that 'every action in the world is temporarily arrested' (*B*

14) and that, when having a fit, he is 'partly an onlooker' (*B* 15) on humanity. Epilepsy, in this way, turns him into a 'truth-machine' (*B* 14) and, using this insanely prophetic gift, he is eventually employed as a detector of forgeries. All of these characteristics, which paradoxically combine a commitment to truth, a sense of detachment, and the mania of a seizure, are those of the novelist. Later on, at a 'time of utter disenchantment' (*B* 111), Ronald challenges the 'company of demons which had been passing through his thoughts. He forced upon their character what attributes of vulnerable grace he could bring to mind' (*B* 112). Here made explicit are the agonizing contradictions for the Sparkian writer. If the imagination is equivalent to 'the devil in [Ronald's] body' then his 'effort of will towards graciousness' (*B* 112) is his abiding struggle to control such demons using the 'vulnerable grace' of fiction. Spark grapples with this mixture of madness and grace, formal control and unruly emotions, in all of her books.

Like many of her exemplary figures, Ronald is a 'different-from' Catholic whose particularity and sickness bars him from becoming a priest. In a key exchange at the beginning of the work, he is told by his 'theological counsellor' why his vocation is not possible: 'A vocation to the priesthood is the will of God. Nothing can change God's will. You are an epileptic. No epileptic can be a priest. *Ergo* you never had a vocation' (*B* 11–12). Such 'retrospective logic', Ronald insists, gives Catholicism a bad name and, later on, he states that 'As a Catholic I loathe all other Catholics' (*B* 79). At the same time, he takes seriously his counsellor's suggestion that he become a 'first rate epileptic' (*B* 11–12). The redemptive qualities of his epilepsy are especially indicated when he has a fit during the night but refuses to take any drugs, so that he could 'get a living troubled sleep instead of a dead and peaceful one' (*B* 87).

The Bachelors, more than anything else, is a novel about the need to make connections, which is why it is crucial that Ronald build bridges between people and different domains. As with *Memento Mori* in relation to old age, this work is brim-full of bachelors, which of necessity raises the acute issue for Spark of the need for human contact and, implicitly, the loneliness and solipsism of the writer. To reinforce Ronald as a transcendent figure, not always recognized by Spark's readers, he encounters

Patrick Seton, an evil double whose surname sounds suspiciously like Satan. Like Ronald, Patrick is a bachelor and also a spiritualist who attempts to act as a medium between distinct spheres. While having a seizure during a seance he is, significantly, physically but not spiritually transformed: 'his eyes opened and turned upward in their sockets. Foam began to bubble at his mouth and faintly trickled down his chin' (B 36). He resembles Robinson in being one of a long line of mythomaniacal figures who mistakenly wish to 'control' (B 124) reality. In Patrick's extreme case, the invention of a private morality finally justifies murder.

The similarities between Ronald and Patrick are used, clearly, to show the extent to which they are moral opposites. After all, while Ronald quests for the truth and is associated with a life-enhancing unity, Patrick commits forgeries and wants to kill his mistress, Alice Dawes. By giving Ronald an obvious double, instead of making his doubleness part of his identity, this book becomes overly didactic and moralistic. Its plot also, with the by now familiar combination of murder, intrigue and blackmail, is rather like a parody of fictional concerns. Spark's equivocation toward the novel form sometimes results in her making everything unreal and contrived. But this refusal to take her work seriously does have its costs. It means that her characters, whose roles are often predetermined by their name, lack autonomy or free will and tend merely to represent a particular narrative viewpoint. In reaction to *The Bachelors*, Spark ironically makes the danger of predestination one of the preoccupations of her next work, *The Prime of Miss Jean Brodie* (1961).

Like *Robinson*, *The Bachelors* is split asunder between body and soul and, in these terms, spiritualism is primarily an extreme form of schism or 'heresy' (B 84). As Ronald's friend Matthew Finch contends, a bogus spiritualism of necessity disavows the 'moral obligations of the flesh' and has 'no sacramental sense' (B 84). Whereas Ronald, through his epilepsy, brings together the natural and the supernatural during his truth-giving seizures, Patrick as a 'dualist' (B 84) splits them apart. Alan Bold also identifies bachelorhood itself, along with homosexuality, as two other false faiths in the book as neither affirm the 'oneness of reality' (B 85).[6] To the extent that being a bachelor or homosexual becomes a fixed identity, outside of the 'moral obligations of the flesh' (*B* 84), it is a form of 'fraudulent conversion' (*B* 109). In *The Comforters*, Caroline regards Ernest Manders, Laurence's uncle, as a 'beautiful hermaphrodite' (*C* 119) and his homosexuality is valued by Helena as it symbolizes his 'differences from the normal' (*C* 122). But in *The Bachelors*, Spark is particularly scathing about Father Mike Socket, a friend of Patrick's, who turns his homosexuality into a cult. As a 'shifty and creedless' (*B* 150) identity, as with Ernest Manders or Marcel Proust, homosexuality is able to challenge received orthodoxies. When, however, it is a 'religion and a Way of Life' (*B* 151), as it is for Father Socket, homosexuality becomes an unreal mythology.

Patrick, who is charged with 'fraudulent conversion', is pointedly described as being 'like a Christian convert of the jungle who secretly returns by night to the fetish tree' (*B* 145) or an originary paganism. Just as homosexuality is both validated as a singular heterodoxy and condemned as a false identity, paganism here is unusually traduced as a spiritualist heresy. In attempting to distinguish absolutely between true and false conversions, Spark in this work believes absolutely in the redemptive promise of religious conversion. But her enduring problem, in her explicitly moralizing fictions, is to represent a Catholic orthodoxy without betraying her imaginative freedom. *Memento Mori* tries to solve this dilemma by crystallizing the supernatural so it has to be faced directly by the author and reader alike. But this, as we have seen, was to overly restrict the autonomy and narrative development of her characters. In response to these constraints, *The Ballad of Peckham Rye* lets singularity run riot and therefore has a refreshingly amoral character at its heart. Unlike *Memento Mori*, this work is wholly on the side of fictional desire. *The Bachelors*, in turn, is a response to the anarchism of *The Ballad of Peckham Rye* but, because of this, is overly prescriptive.

Spark's next three books, published between 1961 and 1965, similarly veer between the desires and freedom of the imagination and the didacticism of a transcendent morality. They also place under scrutiny many of the 'half-worlds' of her past and attempt to transfigure them. Whether set in Edinburgh, London or Jerusalem, her own hybrid life-story and personal history is once again caught between its disruptive singularity and its universalist transformation. The economy of the neo-classical formalist will invariably compete with the emotional pull of the 'fetish tree' or the unconverted past. Now fully matured as a novelist, Spark during the 1960s engages directly with her multiple selves and publishes some of her most creative and lasting achievements.

4

Transfigurations: Edinburgh, London, Jerusalem

The book which most closely resembles *The Prime of Miss Jean Brodie* (1961) is, in many ways, the largely unsung *The Ballad of Peckham Rye*. This comparison is often obscured by the phenomenal success of Spark's sixth novel as a stage-play, feature film and television series. But both works have deceptively attractive and forceful protagonists whose Scottishness defines their difference from convention and helps proclaim their anarchic presence. These determinedly amoral figures paradoxically act as a catalyst to elicit the spiritual life of others. They both exist as witty and alluring personalities who, in a skilful sleight of hand, appear to elude the author's narrative control. Such rampant singularity means that Dougal Douglas and Jean Brodie attempt, not unlike their author, to determine reality. The fact that the figure of Jean Brodie can be so easily extracted from an elaborate and closely textured story-line points to Spark's overpowering fascination with her. That Brodie exists so completely above and beyond the written text is especially startling when we remember that the novel, more than any other to date, is distinguished on the page, as opposed to the stage or screen, by a fragmented and continually shifting narrative.

But as soon as one compares her later and earlier works it becomes clear that *The Prime of Miss Jean Brodie*, along with *The Girls of Slender Means* (1963) and *The Mandelbaum Gate* (1965), have achieved a level of literary sophistication that does eclipse much of what has gone before. Unlike her previous books, Spark now takes absolutely seriously the question of locale and historical context. If her first five novels could easily have been situated anywhere at just about any time, her next three could only have been set in Edinburgh, London and Jerusalem in the 1930s, mid-1940s and early 1960s respectively. They are all related in some way to the history of fascism and the Second World War and its aftermath. What is more, these histories are subtly interwoven into Spark's more abstract moralizing. Whereas her earlier books take specific instances from her past and mythologize them, these later works more thoroughly locate her life-story in time and place so as to explore as fiction many of her past selves and identities. *The Prime of Miss Jean Brodie* also introduces the first sustained use of Spark's distinctive flash-forward technique, to accompany her more conventional use of flash-backs, which complicates any straightforward reading of the novel. As her narrative style becomes more complex, so does the range and depth of her interests.

Where there is continuity between her earlier and later writing is in terms of Spark's abiding sense of death-in-life or of suffering as the foundation of creativity. An important link with both *Memento Mori* and *The Bachelors* is the often stressed fact that Brodie, as a result of the carnage of the First World War, is one of a large number of Edinburgh spinsters and, in broad social terms, is hardly unique:

> It is not to be supposed that Miss Brodie was unique at this point in her prime...She was alone, merely, in that she taught in a school like Marcia Blaine's. There were legions of her kind during the nineteen-thirties, women from the age of thirty upward, who crowded their war-bereaved spinsterhood with voyages of discovery into new ideas and energetic practices in art or social welfare, education or religion. (*PMJB* 42)

Instead of showing humility after the knowledge of death on a mass scale, Brodie acts as if she were immortal, not unlike many of the benighted septuagenarians in *Memento Mori*. What is more, she also weaves unreal fantasies out of her spinsterly solitude, which leads to solipsism and the creation of a private dream-world. But Spark, needless to say, did not call this novel *The Spinsters* after *The Bachelors*. While Brodie might not be 'outwardly odd...inwardly was a different matter...' and it is her deformed 'nature' (*PMJB* 43) which separates her from the legions of lonely Edinburgh spinsters. Her singularity is confined to her internal health and this book, above all else, becomes Brodie's spiritual biography. Even her support for Mussolini and Hitler, in the end, indicates that she was a 'born Fascist' (*PMJB* 125) and that her politics, when compared to her inner deformity, is a 'side interest' (*PMJB* 125).

Halfway through the novel, Sandy Stranger and Jenny Gray gain a crucial insight into Brodie's true character when they listen to yet another account of her 'felled fiancé' (*PMJB* 13) Hugh, who died at Flanders Field. After six years of being taught by Brodie in the junior school (from age 10 to 16) they begin to realize that the story of her dead fiancé has been successively modified over the years. Hugh was always interested in music, reflecting her affair with Gordon Lowther, the school's teacher of song. But in this final retelling Hugh has suddenly become an aficionado of art because of her deeper affection for the art master, Teddy Lloyd, who himself lost an arm during the First World War. Once they realize that Brodie is 'making her new love story fit the old' (*PMJB* 72), Jenny and Sandy listen with 'double ears' and become 'fascinated by this method of making patterns with facts' (*PMJB* 72). Sandy's gradual distrust of Brodie, and the reason for her eventual 'betrayal' (*PMJB* 60) of her beloved teacher, stems from this moment. In the end, Sandy coldly rejects the 'excesses' of Brodie's prime because, in an extreme rendering of Scottish Presbyterianism, she had 'elected herself to grace ... with more exotic suicidal enchantment than if she had simply taken to drink like other spinsters who couldn't stand it any more' (*PMJB* 109).

On one level, Brodie's main offence is that she is a mythomaniac who fictionalizes everything she does as well as those she encounters. This can be seen mainly in her egocentric belief that the six girls who form 'the Brodie set' (*PMJB* 5) can be shaped by her romantic fantasies and fit into her predetermined categories for them. She thus adopts the oft-stated Jesuit belief, which Spark herself deplores, that children are essentially malleable: 'Give me a girl at an impressionable age, and she is mine for life' (*PMJB* 9). This reference to the Jesuits is paradoxical as she is most closely identified with the confining predestination of the Scottish 'God of Calvin, who sees the beginning and the end' (*PMJB* 120). But while Catholicism and Calvinism are contrasted as Sandy Stranger and Jean Brodie,

Rome and Edinburgh, they are not straightforward oppositions. For one thing, we are told that Brodie is 'by temperament suited only to the Roman Catholic Church' which 'could have embraced, even while it disciplined, her soaring and diving spirit' (*PMJB* 85). Brodie's romanticized love for Rome, albeit in secular terms, is an obvious counter to the dour rationalism of the Marcia Blaine School and Presbyterian Edinburgh in general. Sandy Stranger, although a convert to Catholicism, is repeatedly pictured as being imprisoned in her convent clutching at the 'bars of her grille' (*PMJB* 128). What is more, in a parodic version of Spark's usual heroines, she is portrayed as being unpleasantly cerebral and analytical, not unlike a Presbyterian, which Teddy Lloyd deems 'unnatural in a girl of eighteen' (*PMJB* 122). As with much of Spark at her best, the paradoxes of her characters counter overly dogmatic readings of her books.

The comic version of Calvinistic determinism can be found in the self-classifications which each of her girls promotes. Monica Douglas is famous for mathematics and her temper; Rose Stanley is famous for sex; Eunice Gardner is famous for gymnastics and swimming; Jenny Gray is famous for her beauty; Mary Macgregor is famous for being a nobody; and Sandy Stranger is famous for her vowel sounds and 'merely notorious for her small, almost non-existent eyes' (*PMJB* 7). Such categories are amusing when they are merely 'unreal talk' (*PMJB* 119) but become dangerous when Brodie is no longer 'game-planning' (*PMJB* 119) but actually believes her own god-like pretensions. In terms of the God of Calvin, Brodie 'thinks she is Providence' (*PMJB* 120) and that she can therefore mould other people's lives. She thus urges the 'mad' (*PMJB* 118) Joyce Emily Hammond to fight in the Spanish Civil War, where she is killed, and encourages Rose Stanley to sleep with Teddy Lloyd as her surrogate lover. At this point, Sandy decides to put a 'stop' (*PMJB* 125) to Brodie because she is confusing, with lethal consequences, her romantic fantasies with reality.

But the condemnation of Brodie for 'making patterns with facts' (*PMJB* 72) also has a hollow ring to it. After all, such pattern-making is the very essence of the art of fiction. As a writer and artist, respectively, both Sandy and Teddy Lloyd also aestheticize reality, or 'transfigure the commonplace' according to the title of Sandy's 'odd psychological treatise' on the 'nature of moral perception' (*PMJB* 35). To be sure, Brodie does falsely categorize her girls, and much of the plot is about the assertion of their free will, often successfully, in relation to Brodie's intended plans for them. It is also true that her beliefs are often simply an extension of her ego, as can be seen by her typical contention that the 'greatest Italian painter' is Giotto as 'he is my favourite' (*PMJB* 11). But all of these traits – classifying people, transforming life into art, and confusing the self with the world – turns Brodie into a peculiar construct of the novelist. After all, Sandy Stranger is immediately limited and predetermined by her surname – as are so many of Spark's characters – which indicates that she is inevitably estranged; an outsider who is never fully at home in the Brodie set. And the book's narrator, who constantly sees the future and looks back into the past, is more god-like than ever, even though such omniscience is wittily particularized by the use of a rather prim, Edinburgh voice.

In the end, what distinguishes this work is its refusal to make easy moral judgements. David Lodge overstates the case when he describes this 'largely comic novel' as containing a 'severe and uncompromising dogmatic message'.[1] In this reading, Brodie is a bogus Christ-figure and the Brodie set a caricature of the 'chosen' (*PMJB* 79) or the Christian apostles. The Church as the mystical body of Christ is travestied, according to Lodge, when Sandy looks back at her companions and 'understood them as a body with Miss Brodie as a head' (*PMJB* 30). Teddy Lloyd is aware of this symbolism when he paints all of the Brodie girls as if they were versions of Jean Brodie. When he offers to paint a group portrait, Sandy comments tellingly that the girls would 'look like one big Miss Brodie, I suppose' (*PMJB* 102). Such specious messianism, in this work, leads to fascism which is an extreme account of a single body with the head of a redemptive leader. In *Memento Mori*, the eleven 'grannies' in the Maud Long Medical Ward lie 'still and soundless breathing like one body' (*MM* 116) and, as completely spiritual beings, are a sympathetic instance of the same theological symbolism. But, unlike her earlier work, Spark now leaves it up to the reader to decide which is the true and which the false rendition of her ambiguous moral universe.

The abiding problem with Lodge's orthodox reading of *The Prime of Miss Jean Brodie* is that it fails to account sufficiently for the many paradoxes in the novel which are reinforced by its dislocated narrative. On a didactic level, Sandy rejects Brodie as a false Christ-figure and converts to the real thing by becoming a Catholic nun called Sister Helena of the Transfiguration. The shift from Calvinist predestination to the centrality of free will within Catholicism points to a blunt theological divide. But, as we have seen, such easy oppositions are subverted in this work because Spark sets up many possible readings of her main characters, with each interpretation being equally plausible. Both Brodie and Sandy have strong and competing elements of Calvinism and Catholicism within them. It is misleading, in these terms, to place Sandy at the moral centre of this work as so many critics have done. Much of the action is seen through Sandy's narrow 'little pig-like eyes' (*PMJB* 66) which are repeatedly described as 'almost non-existent' (*PMJB* 7). While Brodie has an excess of vision Sandy, in stark contrast, almost literally lacks vision.

One of Brodie's many contradictions is that, for all her crypto-fascist control of her girls, she hates anything that smacks of 'the team spirit' (*PMJB* 78), which is authoritarian and diminishes their individuality. After all, Brodie's definition of education is, 'a leading out', 'from *ex*, out, and *duco*, I lead' (*PMJB* 36). This is an essentially liberal version of education from below as opposed to the imposition of knowledge on her pupils from above. But, *ex duco*, of course, is similar to Il Duce, the title which Mussolini adopted. Brodie, in these terms is something of a liberal cliché – the free-thinking schoolteacher who inspires her pupil – and Spark clearly wanted to subvert such easy approval. The unattractive Sandy, on the other hand, is a rather monodimensional figure as suggested by her allegorical surname, Stranger, even though she is ostensibly supposed to embody the novel's truths. While Sandy's crisis of belief and coming of age drives the action of the plot, we gain very little insight into her reasons for her conversion and we know absolutely nothing about her 'odd psychological treatise' (*PMJB* 35) except that it finally made her famous.

As Bernard Harrison rightly argues, the story-line might well be organized around Sandy but she remains 'enigmatic and incomplete' and is treated throughout as if she were a rather peripheral figure.[2] In Spark's previous works, monodimensional characters without any inner life were automatically dismissed as moral degenerates. Sandy, however, is both a disagreeable caricature and close to being an authorial mouthpiece. She is half-English, like Spark, a 'stranger' to Edinburgh, and has a 'creeping vision of disorder' (*PMJB* 86) which her conversion is meant to resolve. As well as being close to Spark in terms of her life-history, she is the most unlovable of heroines, and when she dismisses Brodie as a 'tiresome woman' (*PMJB* 60) the reader's sympathy is undoubtedly on the side of her more seductive and nuanced teacher. Like Douglas, Brodie is both attractive and dangerous and impossible, finally, to pin down. By the end, she is most closely identified with her famous ancestor, Deacon William Brodie, a respectable 'man of substance' (*PMJB* 88) who was a 'night burglar', a bigamist, and died 'cheerfully on a gibbet of his own devising' (*PMJB* 88). As Velma Richmond has noted, William Brodie was the historical source for Robert Louis Stevenson's *The Strange Tale of Dr Jekyll and Mr Hyde* (1886) which is also centrally concerned with the doubleness of its protagonist.[3]

Above all else, this novel resists an easy transcendence which has hitherto distinguished Spark's work. In *The Ballad of Peckham Rye* there is a vision of Peckham which ends the book and points to 'another world than this' with the Rye 'looking like a cloud of green and gold, the people seeming to ride upon it' (*BPR* 143). There is no such closure in *The Prime of Miss Jean Brodie* but, instead, Edinburgh is viewed in passing as a 'floating city when the light was a special pearly white' (*PMJB* 111). This, however, is just one of a large number of versions of the city and of Brodie who looked 'beautiful and fragile' in this light (*PMJB* 111). Spark, for the first time, resists using a definitive voice to give an ultimate or complete meaning to events or characters. Thus, Sandy ends the novel by repeating the anticlimactic refrain that 'Miss Jean Brodie in her prime' (*PMJB* 128) was an important influence on her. But we know from what has gone before, that Brodie's prime – 'Prime what?' (*PMJB* 27) – is a particularly vague notion as it is both a noun and an adjective. In a typical paradox, Brodie herself objects to exactly this kind of linguistic vagueness: 'Social what?', she responds, when one of her girls says that she is going to 'a social' (*PMJB* 62).

The Prime of Miss Jean Brodie is a deliberately uncertain rendition of a figure who is defined *par excellence* by her astonishing, if misplaced, certainties. The reason why Sandy's famous treatise, 'The Transfiguration of the Commonplace', is left unexplained is that Spark allows her readers to tease out the truth about Brodie and engage in the act of transformation themselves. Like Brodie's view of education, Spark does not wish to impose meaning on her novel from above, but leaves 'the nature of moral perception' (*PMJB* 35) to her individual readers. Her next novel, *The Girls of Slender Means* (1963), explores another spurious world of innocence where a mistakenly idealized female community is shown to have an underlying 'savagery' (*GSM* 60). Not unlike the Marcia Blaine School, the May of Teck Club provides Spark with a circumscribed social grouping which she can simultaneously document, mythologize and debunk. The May of Teck Club is a genteel lodging house for impoverished young women situated in Kensington, near the Albert Memorial. This residence again provides a limited but symbolic focus through which a wider history, the immediate aftermath of the Second World War, can be delineated.

The central figure in the book, Nicholas Farringdon, is principally recalled in flash-backs and, like Sandy, he is strangely marginalized as his consciousness and reasoning has to be reconstructed by the reader. He is also the novel's memento mori, as much of the plot revolves around Jane Wright, a 'woman columnist' (*GSM* 9) engaged in 'brain-work' (*GSM* 37), who informs ex-members of the club that he has died recently. Nicholas's death literally haunts the novel and he becomes an absent presence who, while at the heart of the story-line, is removed from the present-day narrative both spatially and temporally. Just as Jean Brodie is assessed through the quizzical future gaze of Sandy, the May of Teck Club comes under Nicholas's posthumous sceptical scrutiny. Much of *The Girls of Slender Means* concerns the reasons for Nicholas's conversion to Catholicism; a self-transfiguration which usually characterizes Spark's early heroines. While Sandy had to debunk the unreal and anarchic world of Jean Brodie, Nicholas has to banish his male fantasies concerning the purity of the May of Teck Club. After introducing Colonel Felix Dobell to the club, the book's female narrator notes the conventional male reaction to this community of women:

> The Colonel seemed to be in love with the entire club...This was a common effect on its male visitors, and Nicholas was enamoured of the entity in only one exceptional way, that it stirred his poetic sense to the point of exasperation, for at the same time he discerned with irony the process of his own thoughts, how he was imposing upon this society an image incomprehensible to itself. (*GSM* 71)

Nicholas is a masculine rendition of Spark's independent-minded personae, and would-be converts, who are able to view the world with irony and to distinguish truth from unreality. A deliberately whimsical and self-contradictory figure, Nicholas begins as an anarchist poet and ends as a Catholic missionary in Haiti. At one point he is said to be undecided 'whether to live in England or France' or 'whether he preferred men or women' since he 'alternated' (*GSM* 53) with both. He also could not 'make up his mind between suicide and an equally drastic course of action known as Father D'Arcy' (*GSM* 53). A pacifist, he joins the army at the outbreak of war as he believes that this will bring about peace. Although he consistently describes himself as an anarchist, he dislikes most other anarchists (*GSM* 69). Nicholas, in other words, is the epitome of indeterminacy who is able to unify a range of opposing forces. His problem is that he, initially, wishes to resolve his uncertainties by imagining the May of Teck Club as a 'microcosmic ideal society' (*GSM* 65). Even though he realizes that he was imposing a false 'poetic image' (*GSM* 65) on the club, this idea continues to torment him and culminates in his love for the 'exceedingly beautiful' (*GSM* 31) Selina Redwood.

As her name suggests, Selina is a force of nature whose first name might be said to derive from the Greek for moon.[4] But, in contrast to Spark's usually sympathetic lunar-loving pagans, Selina is like the dark side of the moon, cold, remote and indifferent. On a doctrinaire level, Spark wanted to subvert the conventional image of female innocence which confuses disastrously the beauty of youth with moral virtue. Although others, such as Jane Wright, have a more jaundiced and realistic perception of their time at the May of Teck, Nicholas insists on thinking of the club as a 'community held together by the graceful attributes of common poverty' (*GSM* 84–5). But this materialist conception of grace is essentially false as it confuses the lack of wealth of 'the girls of slender means' with their internal health. Selina, especially, is a parody of genuine grace in her oft-repeated 'Two Sentences' which begin, 'Poise is perfect balance, an equanimity of body and mind' (*GSM* 50). Spark satirizes mercilessly this form of physical grace, which was learnt from the 'Chief Instructress of the Poise Course', as Selina believes that she will achieve equanimity simply by repeating her mantra twice daily.

Nicholas's materialist fallacy is consummated when he, 'with the reckless ambition of a visionary' (*GSM* 92), passionately desires Selina as if her hollow words could have an inner meaning. While recognising her narcissism and egocentricity, he sleeps with her with the 'aim of converting her soul' (*GSM* 92) so that he might, in god-like fashion, bring about her transfiguration. His confusion of inner and outer beauty is finally shattered, however, when he witnesses her, after the May of Teck Club is set ablaze by an unexploded bomb, saving a Schiaparelli dress rather than any of her friends. At this point he realizes that 'nowhere's safe' (*GSM* 125) and that a 'vision of evil may be as effective to conversion as a vision of good' (*GSM* 140). With typical Sparkian poetic justice, it is he who is finally converted by Selina. Rather didactically, Nicholas learns the error of his ways and, unlike Spark's many other self-deluded characters, he is unusually rewarded for attempting to make reality conform to his fantasies.

There is a stark contrast between the physical prowess of Selina and the romantic sensibility of Joanna Childe who, as her surname suggests, naively believes that 'all...ideas of love and honour came from the poets' (*GSM* 22). Joanna is an elocution teacher who we frequently hear reciting lines of poetry which have an oblique relation to the action of the novel. Gerard Manley Hopkins's 'Wreck of the Deutschland', which resonates throughout, prefigures the disastrous fate of the May of Teck Club, and the nun in the poem anticipates the equally virginal Joanna's misfortune. Lines from Coleridge's 'Kubla Khan' also highlight the presence of evil in a place where it is supposedly meant to be absent. But it would be wrong to think of Joanna simply as the moral opposite of Selina as some readers have argued.[5] If Selina is the embodiment of the physical world, then Joanna is sometimes quite literally a disembodied human voice who is detached completely from what is palpable. Both women, in other words, are considered to be situated wholly in either the material or spiritual domain. Nicholas pointedly comments on Joanna that for her 'Poetry takes the place of sex' (*GSM* 80), which clearly illustrates her mistaken conflation of image and actuality.

It is by now familiar Sparkian territory that the extremes of both Selina's materialism and Joanna's spirituality are equally dangerous as they deny the sacramental combination of both. Where *The Girls of Slender Means* becomes rather too dogmatic is in portraying Nicholas as the ideal synthesis of vision and action. His conversion, rather like Sandy's neat resolution of her 'creeping vision of disorder' (*PMJB* 86), transcends his contradictory nature a little too easily. Spark is not interested in detailing her characters' motives and she therefore leaves the reasons for their conversion as a mystery for her readers to decipher. But if such choices are too quickly smoothed over, leaving a conversionist orthodoxy effortlessly in place, then her redeemed protagonists become flattened and allegorical. With typical perversity, Spark's seventh book regards 1945, or the 'year of final reckoning' (*GSM* 8), as an erroneous reawakening which is reduced to political electioneering and the distorted emotions of the masses. The extreme violence and hysteria which accompany the VE and VJ celebrations point to a time when, after years of public conflict, there is a lack of any inner resources to cope with entirely private struggles. But, at the same time as Spark denies the restorative significance of the post-war era as a whole, she is in danger of portraying her fictionalized Catholic converts as uniquely possessing a sense of equanimity.

Near the beginning of *The Girls of Slender Means*, Spark's somewhat cynical narrator imagines an 'organic' crowd, celebrating the defeat of Nazi Germany, as made up of 'strange arms...twined around strange bodies': 'Many liaisons, some permanent, were formed in the night, and numerous infants of experimental variety, delightful in hue of skin and racial structure, were born to the world...nine months after' (*GSM* 17). As always, Spark seems unsure of the value of these uncontrollable passions which resulted in such hybrid types. But her own sense of hybridity, and self-confessed obsessiveness when writing a novel, clearly gives her a unique insight and empathy with such unbridled emotions. Her next book, *The*

Mandelbaum Gate (1965), explores the fear and desire inherent in this disruptive racial singularity, which is given a historical resonance with reference to the Nazi doctrine of expunging such differences.

Set in a bifurcated Jerusalem in 1961, *The Mandelbaum Gate* is unique among Spark's oeuvre in relation to both its subject matter and its literary form. It is her only novel to explore in depth her Gentile–Jewish background although this is alluded to in many of her other works. What is more, especially in contrast to her previous two books, it is her longest, least serene and most ambitious novel to date. Spark clearly felt compelled to understand a key aspect of her past that, as with Sandy and Nicholas at their most agonized, had continued to haunt her long after her conversion. For this reason, Spark's eighth novel has been described as heterodox and anarchic with an 'untidy and crowded' cast of misfits.[6] The eponymous Mandelbaum Gate is quite literally a piece of no-man's-land between the Jordanian and Israeli sides of Jerusalem. This in-between setting illustrates the extent to which Spark now wished to examine, on a grand scale, her fundamental preoccupations concerning the divisions and unities at the core of her own identity.

As we have seen, Spark had an ambivalent relation to her part-Jewishness, as it was initially associated with the madness and disorder of her life before her conversion. In *The Comforters*, Jewishness is dismissed as one of Caroline Rose's 'half-worlds' (*C* 48) which needed to be transcended. Caroline's Jewish family is also viewed as having an unreal sense of themselves, like Mrs Georgina Hogg, as one of the suffering. By the time of *Memento Mori*, a Mr and Mrs Rose (perhaps related to Caroline) are introduced as part of an elderly group of people who visit Henry Mortimer in the hope that he will solve the mystery of the anonymous telephone caller. Both have stereotypical Jewish characteristics which is unsurprising in a novel largely made up of caricatures. Mr Rose is called at his 'business premises' (*MM* 149) and spreads 'wide his palms' (*MM* 152) when talking to Henry. Mrs Rose has 'longanimous eyes and resignation' and nods 'her head in sad, wise and ancient assent' (*MM* 152) in reaction to Henry's philosophizing. Both are realists and, in the context of an assembly of egotistical escapists, are largely sympathetic because of their honesty. Mr Rose, in fact, inadvertently speaks the truth when he asks 'who's the fellow that's trying to put the fear of God into us?' (*MM* 152). Not unlike his wife, he too has an unconscious access to the ancient wisdom of the past.

The Jerusalem locale of *The Mandelbaum Gate* allows Spark to value her part-Jewishness as a sign of her uniqueness as a 'different-from' Catholic. By leaving England, her heroine, Barbara Vaughan, is also given a good deal of sexual freedom, with Jewishness, throughout the novel, directly associated with Barbara's 'sexual instincts' (*MG* 43). In fact, up until the end of this work, Barbara was prepared to marry and sleep with a Protestant divorcee. For most of its composition, after a two-month trip to Jerusalem in 1961, this book was known as 'The Gentile Jewesses', which, as we have seen, was to become a separate quasi-autobiographical story. Jewishness, in these terms, was depicted primarily as an uncategorizable identity which disrupts the usual conventions. But, as in the case of Dougal Douglas or Jean Brodie, Spark has an equivocal attitude to such singular identities. After all, singularity can be both an expression of free will and a means of evading immutable truths which necessarily supersedes human particularity. Male homosexuality, for instance, is both valued and denigrated by Spark: for being unconventional in *The Comforters* and an ersatz religion in *The Bachelors*. But, in the expansive mood of *The Mandelbaum Gate*, Jews and Judaism remain anarchic and disruptive. Spark no longer regards such differences as a threat, as they help the reader to question orthodox religious or national groupings of all kinds.

The connection between content and form in this novel is particularly worth stressing. There is a strong link between Spark's books which exert a tight narrative control over her characters and the attempt to subsume the past within a transcendent theology. In stark contrast, history and her central figures all have a dangerous autonomy in *The Mandelbaum Gate* and self-consciously escape Spark's distinctive aesthetic command. Jewishness, in other words, represents a kind of freedom which is reflected in the unusual exuberance of her writing. After all, Spark spent two years composing this book as compared to, say, the eight weeks which she took over *The Prime of Miss Jean Brodie*. It became her bulkiest work, closer than any of her others to the sprawling English realist tradition of George Eliot and E. M. Forster. Spark acknowledged its significance at the time by describing it on publication as 'a very important book for me, much more concrete and solidly rooted in a very detailed setting' than what had gone before. But, in a later interview, she rejected the book because it remained outside of her narrative control: 'I don't like that book awfully much...it's out of proportion. In the beginning it's slow, and in the end it's very rapid, it races...I got bored, because it is too long, so I decided never again to write a long book, keep them short'.[7] Given its unrestrained form and Jewish subject matter, it is not surprising that this work should continue to disturb Spark long after it was written.

The transition from Sandy Stranger to Barbara Vaughan, both partial versions of Spark, gives a clear indication of how radically her aesthetic had changed in *The Mandelbaum Gate*. Whereas Sandy Stranger's consciousness had to be recreated by her readers, the scrupulously charted split identity of Barbara Vaughan reverberates throughout the novel. Appropriately enough, the second chapter of *The Mandelbaum Gate* is called 'Barbara Vaughan's Identity' and it is her self-confessed 'state of conflict' (*MG* 23) which extends into the polarized history of the Middle East and the bisected city of Jerusalem. The eponymous Mandelbaum Gate, which acts as a crossing-point 'from Jerusalem to Jerusalem' (*MG* 9), makes it possible for Barbara to move within and between identities. No longer a cipher in relation to a higher moral order, Barbara's sense of anarchism and disorder, unlike that of Sandy and Nicholas, is not short-lived. To maintain this sense of disruption, all the seemingly straightforward figures in this book act against type. These include Freddie Hamilton, the 'lukewarm' (*MG* 21) racist English diplomat, who eventually becomes the impulsive saviour of Barbara. Most notable also in this regard is Miss Rickward, the quasi-lesbian headmistress of Barbara's school, who has a passionate affair with Joe Ramdez. In a radically divided world, the search for unity is not an act of god-like transfiguration imposed from above, but begins with the singular differences of Spark's characters.

From the beginning, Barbara argues that 'the essential thing about herself remained unspoken, uncategorized, unlocated'

(*MG* 28) and later she makes explicit her credo: 'There's always more to it than Jew, Gentile, half-Jew, half-Gentile. There's the human soul, the individual. Not "Jew, Gentile" as one might say "autumn, winter". Something unique and unrepeatable' (*MG* 37). When pressed to identify herself unequivocally as a Jew by her Israeli tour guide, Barbara replies in the spirit of such unique transfiguration: 'I am who I am' (*MG* 28) which ironically echoes God's answer to Moses from the burning bush on Mount Sinai. And yet, she soon becomes anxious at such 'mysterious truths', which 'were all right for deathbed definitions, when one's mental obligations were at an end' (*MG* 29). Barbara's welcome intellectual scepticism can be contrasted with Father Jerome, the Catholic priest who, with god-like authority, tells Caroline Rose in *The Comforters* that 'she was as she was' (*C* 62). Unlike Caroline, who welcomes the mystification of her identity, Barbara is well aware that the effortless transformation of such ethnic, cultural and religious particularities, especially in the context of the Middle East, becomes a too easy form of 'escape' (*MG* 31). She questions an unthinking transcendence, as well as the Israeli tour guide's demand for definition which, she believes, resembles the false 'territorial consciousness' of other historically powerless peoples such as the Scots, the Irish and the Welsh (*MG* 29).

By refusing either to territorialize her racial difference, or to transcend it, Barbara Vaughan stands outside of both a dominant nationalism and an orthodox conversionism. What is more, her Gentile Jewishness becomes a model for other anarchic unplaceable individuals throughout the novel. Barbara is attracted to her lover, Harry Clegg, for instance, as he eludes the unspoken assumption which pigeonholes him as an 'Englishman of lower-class origin' or 'red-brick genius' (*MG* 41). The eroticizing of her Jewishness similarly qualifies her role as an 'English spinster' and she thinks of hers and Harry's refusal to be typecast as an 'equivalent quality' (*MG* 41). The novel is, in fact, stuffed full of people, such as Abdul and Suzi Ramdez, who cannot be addressed in a conventional mode. In the end, these identity-less individuals all seem to break down commonplace assumptions about nation, gender and class and can be said to form an alternative community of exiles. Spark is quite explicit about this in her account of the blue-eyed, dark-skinned Palestinian brother and sister, Abdul and Suzi, who 'belonged to nothing but themselves' (*MG* 101) and yet, paradoxically, are part of a group made up of

> lapsed Jews, lapsed Arabs, lapsed citizens, runaway Englishmen, dancing prostitutes, international messes, failed painters, intellectuals, homosexuals. Some were silent, some voluble. Some were mentally ill, or would become so. (*MG* 101)

The warning at the end of this quotation that 'some were mentally ill, or would become so', reminds the reader of the price that, as with Spark's own breakdown, might be paid for such radical dislocation. At the same time, immediately after this paragraph, the narrative voice intervenes to repeat unequivocally that 'others were not [mad], and never would become so; and would have been the flower of the Middle East, given the sun and air of the mind not yet available' (*MG* 101). Such is the thin line between madness and prophecy which Spark was to be increasingly concerned with. Earlier in the chapter, we are told that Abdul Ramdez categorized those in power as 'the System', which included 'fathers, the Pope, President Nasser, King Hussein, Mr Ben-Gurion, the Grand Mufti, the Patriarch of Jerusalem, the English Sovereign, the civil servants and upper militia throughout the world' (*MG* 81). His opposition to 'the System', essentially patriarchal power, is both a form of lunacy and a revolutionary new way of imagining the Middle East. Spark, throughout *The Mandelbaum Gate*, is at pains to oppose orthodoxies of all kinds in these prophetic terms.

In fact, her preoccupation with madness as a form of creative disordering refers back to 'The Gentile Jewesses', which opens with the grandmother frightening away a 'madman' (*CS* 308) from the local asylum who threatened to murder her in her shop. The story of this lunatic in turn unlocks other, equally disruptive, forms of anarchy and refers implicitly to the mother's devotion to the lunar calendar in 'The Gentile Jewesses'. Barbara, importantly, 'caught some of Freddy's madness' when she eventually felt herself to be 'all of a piece; Gentile and Jewess, Vaughan and Aaronson ... a private-judging Catholic, a shy adventuress' (*MG* 164). At this point, Freddy's madness enables her to accept her manifold singularity. Spark's account, in general, of the English abroad in Israel and Jordan also allows the reader to question the stability and assumptions of any particular identity. When Barbara illegally scatters flower-seeds across national boundaries, as Jacqueline Rose has noted, there is a sense in which she is being both proprietorial and irreverent. Englishness, in these terms, simultaneously represents a kind of freedom as well as a parodic rehash of colonialism.[8] All of the multiple identities in the novel are, in this way, difficult to contain, as they are equally both liberating and a form of potentially disabling madness.

In a bid to resolve the ambivalence of these unplaceable identities, Barbara often yearns for the transformation of all differences. When on Mount Tabor, she misquotes Dante who, she believes, wished to bind the Old and New Testaments 'by love into one volume' (*MG* 26). Later on, by the Basilica of the Transfiguration, she stresses that, even though Mount Hermon might be the place where Christ was redeemed, she still believes in his transfiguration 'in a radiant time of metamorphosis...-white and dazzling' (*MG* 48). Freddy's madness also results in his disappearing for three days soon after the Feast of Transfiguration. In an important set-piece sermon, Spark has an unorthodox priest bring together the conviction of faith with the truth of architectural history. This vision of synthesizing opposites, especially apocrypha and history, reflects Barbara's equally irrational desire to transfigure her experience into a new whole while affirming her unique difference.

The split in Barbara's janus-faced identity is writ large in the historical backdrop of the novel when it comes to the account of the Eichmann trial. In stark contrast to Barbara's 'unique and unrepeatable' sense of self, Eichmann represents the ultimate determinist and false categorizer who drains people of their uniqueness. Barbara's response to the trial is to see Eichmann as essentially a false convert whose perverse beliefs are held with utter conviction. As Gabriel Josipovici has noted, Spark characterizes evil as a form of 'self-love and self-righteousness which goes with the refusal of the imagination'.[9] To this extent, Eichmann becomes a ghastly version of a bad novelist:

> Barbara felt she was caught in a conspiracy to prevent her brain from functioning.... The man was plainly not testifying for himself, but for his pre-written destiny. He was not answering for himself or his own life at all, but for an imperative deity named Bureau IV-B-4, of

whom he was the High Priest. (*MG* 179)

The Eichmann trial exposes not only the dangers of holding an absolute faith but also the impossible attempt to contain the particularities of history within Barbara's conflicted sense of transcendence. During the trial, she is reminded rather solipsistically of her schooling, where she read the French *nouveau roman* or 'anti-novel' and thought of 'repetition, boredom, despair, going nowhere for nothing, all of which conditions are enclosed in a tight, unbreakable statement of the times at hand' (*MG* 177). In an anticipation of Hannah Arendt's famous description of Eichmann's testimony as 'the banality of evil', the judges presiding over the trial all bear the 'recognizable scars of the western intellectual' (*MG* 178).[10] But Eichmann is also the very real product of European history which cannot be easily transformed into Barbara's search for meaning outside of the specificities of these events. For this reason, the scenes concerning Eichmann include Spark's verbatim transcriptions of the trial, as if nothing can be added to the historical record. *The Mandelbaum Gate* attempts to aestheticize history but, at the same time, is forced to acknowledge the impossibility of this imaginative conversion.

The Mandelbaum Gate undoubtedly marked an important turning point in Spark's career as a novelist as it was her most comprehensive attempt to convert life into art. Up until this point, Spark had examined aspects of her early history and personal formation which culminated in her conversion. Her writing, in these terms, was knowingly redemptive; a means of transfiguring the half-worlds of Presbyterian Edinburgh or of bohemian London. The Eichmann trial, above all else, compelled Spark to question the belief in the value of an absolutist transfiguration. It is perhaps in horrified reaction to Eichmann as the parodic double of a true believer that Spark, after this novel, was to construct a world which was to remain radically unconverted.

The unconverted self, in the light of the doctrine of original sin, is complicit with evil, whereas, from a novelist's viewpoint, it is immensely seductive as essential source material. This unresolved love–hate relation with the imaginative arts reaches its climax in *The Mandelbaum Gate* with its heterodox validation of unchangeable and anarchic individualism and the creative madness which arises from this. After her most Jewish book, Spark was never again to place herself in a position where she was unable to convert her life-history into a transfigured narrative. In her next three works, Spark moves as far away as she possibly can from the historical detail and scope of her eighth novel. While some critics regard *The Mandelbaum Gate* as a blind alley, because it was so vehemently rejected by her, we shall see that it was to be a prototype for the later novels of Spark's output. For the time being, however, it is a model merely of the kind of book which was to be completely exorcized over most of the next decade.

5

Machine-Made Parables: From Satire to Absurdity

Muriel Spark's next three books, considered among her very best, are written in reaction to *The Mandelbaum Gate* and her other baggier works such as *The Comforters*, *Robinson* and *The Bachelors*. Spark's dislike of *The Mandelbaum Gate*, expressed in her 1970 interview, particularly concerned its panoramic scope and ensuing lack of authorial direction. But her rejection of this looser documentary form in her subsequent short parables – *The Public Image* (1968), *The Driver's Seat* (1970) and *Not to Disturb* (1971) – is also a direct response to her prolonged exploration of her past. Spark, in these new works, is no longer interested in the consciousness or life-story of the individual nor in the virtues of historical reconstruction. Her foreshortened fictional world is now decidedly minimalist with a callous indifference to its inhabitants, who only rarely manage to break free from their external circumstances.

On one level, these three books are merely a return to the concise mode and impersonal, aloof voice of her earlier novellas such as *Memento Mori*, *The Prime of Miss Jean Brodie* and *The Girls of Slender Means*. But her later works differ from their predecessors in having a cool and uncluttered surface which is the least messy, the least emotionally invested, of Spark's writings. At this stage in her career Spark was especially influenced by the French *nouveau roman* and the work of Alain Robbe-Grillet. In *The Mandelbaum Gate*, Barbara Vaughan had associated the *nouveau roman* or 'anti-novel' (*MG* 177) with the testimony of Adolf Eichmann. Eichmann, like the authors of the anti-novel, turns people into objects and drains them of their humanity by using a deadening bureaucratic language. Spark, in this light, utilizes the anti-novel as a means of substituting conventional concerns with the inner self for a more chilling and dehumanized account of the 'times at hand' (*MG* 177).

Up until *The Takeover* (1976) Spark simply gave up on material – either historical or personal – which could not be completely ordered and contained. In these new works there is a distinct shift from actuality to artifice, from the past to the present, and to a pitiless tone which has been rightly described, in relation to her earlier output, as 'machine made'.[1] Angus Wilson, who used this prescient phrase, was commenting on the difference between *The Mandelbaum Gate* and what had gone before. But it is not a coincidence that many of Spark's novels of this time are dominated by machines of all kinds such as aeroplanes, automobiles, cameras, tape-recorders, telephones, food-processors, air-conditioners and sophisticated surveillance and propaganda equipment. Spark, at her best, has shown that the themes of her novels dictate their form and there is a crucial link here between her heartless 'machine made' tone and her highly mechanized creations.

Spark's key 1970 essay, 'The Desegregation of Art', acts as a manifesto for her fiction of this period and also points to the need, in the name of literary satire, for 'less emotion and more intelligence' (DA 25):

> the art and literature of sentiment and emotion, however beautiful in itself, however striking in its depiction of actuality, has to go. It cheats us into a sense of involvement with life and society, but in reality it is a segregated activity. In its place I advocate the arts of satire and ridicule. And I see no other living art form in the future. (DA 24)

There is, on one level, nothing new in this statement as Spark has always considered herself to be a satirist. In her 1961 essay 'My Conversion', for instance, she argues that her new-found faith 'gave her something to work on as a satirist' as it was a 'norm from which one can depart' (MC 60). Spark's sense of religious orthodoxy meant initially that her use of caricature, as in *Memento Mori*, always had an underlying ethical framework. By the time of 'The Desegregation of Art', however, Spark has become less a satirist than an absurdist who no longer allows moral truths to facilely underpin her sense of a corrupt world.

She makes this clear in a 1970 interview, later repeated in *The Hothouse by the East River* (1973), where she states that she does not 'believe in good and evil so much any more' but in 'absurdity and intelligence'.[2] Her move from a moralizing satirist to an amoral absurdist is signalled in 'The Desegregation of Art' with particular regard to the rise of Nazism:

> We have all seen on the television those documentaries of the thirties and of the Second World War, where Hitler and his goose-stepping troops advance in their course of liberating, as they called it, some country or other; we have seen the strutting and posturing of Mussolini. It looks like something out of comic opera to us. If the massed populations of those countries had been moved to break up in helpless laughter at the sight, those tyrants wouldn't have had a chance. And I say we should all be conditioned and educated to regard violence in any form as something to be ruthlessly mocked. (DA 24)

Spark contrasts the ruthless mockery of fascist dictators with what she calls, with extraordinary prescience, the prevailing 'cult of the victim' (DA 24). She believes that the representation of the victim, even in the 'dramatic portrayal of the gross racial injustices of our world' (DA 23), results in a banal emotional catharsis which leaves society essentially unchanged. As early as *The Comforters*, as we have seen, Caroline Rose had been repelled by the 'fireside martyrs, Jews and Catholics' who thought of themselves as 'the Chosen' largely because they were 'infatuated with a tragic sense of themselves' (*C* 38). But, unlike Caroline, who retreats from society at the end of *The Comforters*, Spark now wishes to transcend a self-aggrandizing 'victim-oppressor complex' by using the more resonant and worldly 'arts of satire and ridicule' (DA 23–4).

Unlike the sinister and disabling presence of Eichmann in Jerusalem, Spark's desegregated vision, and sense of absurdity, transcends the segregated particularities of 'racial injustices'. Rather than focusing on the suffering of a specific group of victims, which segregates the artist from the world, Spark stresses a more holistic undertaking where her 'deliberate cunning' and 'derisive...intelligence' can change the 'minds and hearts' of everyone (DA 25). As with the more orthodox view of conversion – as a complete transfiguration of irrationality and disorder – Spark, in this essay, wishes to go beyond the messy emotional response of those who become 'indignant' at 'social injustice' (DA 25). Instead of making her subject a particular set of grievances, Spark romantically desires the 'art form itself' to 'cry...to heaven for vengeance' (DA 26). This characteristic quest for wholeness, and aesthetic transcendence, no longer takes the moralizing form of absorption into the Catholic Church. What is most significant about reframing the contemporary cult of victimhood in the universalizing language of artistic intelligence is that it is explicitly amoral. For this reason, Spark's essay calls for the 'intelligent sacrifice of good things at the intelligent season and by intelligent methods' and rejects the study of evil as a 'banal moral precept' (DA 23).

The Public Image (1968) is the first of Spark's absurdist parables where the desegregated writer is particularly effective in changing her decidedly unsympathetic anti-heroine. This work above all illustrates the 'sacrifice of good things' for the sake of a higher (not necessarily god-like) intelligence. Primarily subject to the art of ridicule Annabel Christopher, the chief protagonist of *The Public Image*, is a third-rate film actress who has been speciously remade by her 'public image' (*PI* 7) into an 'English Tiger-Lady' (*PI* 6). Annabel, in this way, is almost wholly determined by other people's fantasies. Spark's language, echoing her heroine's anxieties, sounds decidedly neurotic. The 'narrow streets within narrower' (*PI* 60) of bohemian Rome reflect the rather entangled view of the world of the book's cosmopolitan elite. After all, Annabel, in striving to establish herself as an international film actress, is, in paranoid fashion, constantly on the lookout for anything that will damage her public image. Locked into an unnatural and inhuman domain, she is absolutely deprived of any authorial compassion.

In a parody of Spark's erstwhile unifying figures, Annabel's mythical identity as a Tiger-Lady combines the erotic passion of a tiger with the chill decorum of an English lady. This fusion is, to some extent, a pastiche of the Gentile Jewess, Barbara Vaughan, whose contradictory identity also brings together the gentility of an 'English spinster' (*MG* 41) with the reputed 'sexual instincts' (*MG* 43) of the Jewess. But it would be wrong to think of Annabel as simply continuous with Spark's previous heroines. On the contrary, the truth-telling attributes of a

Caroline Rose or a Barbara Vaughan are now replaced by the folly of those less well endowed with insight or intelligence. Unlike Caroline and Barbara's acute self-knowledge, Annabel has a 'deep core of stupidity that... thrives on the absence of a looking glass' (*PI* 9). In an unmistakable comparison with these former personae, Annabel has become an anti-heroine to match the form of *The Public Image* as an anti-novel. With a knowing hardness, Spark's fiction has clearly given up on any notion of human agency or authenticity. The earlier more rounded figures are now flattened out and have become, instead, an impersonal anti-self defined by the absence of consciousness. That is why Annabel needs to hold on to her public image to 'pin-point her mind in every precise way, lest it should give way to turmoil' (*PI* 99). It is no longer the truth which can prevent madness but rather, in an extreme reversal, a paranoid fantasy which is used to conceal the truth.

Annabel's chimerical world is finally shattered when her jealous and displaced husband, Frederick Christopher, commits suicide after circulating a series of damaging letters which attempt to unmake her public image. Frederick, in other words, becomes the amoral authorial intelligence which enables Annabel to grope towards a sense of reality. At the point at which he martyrs himself, in the caves under the Church of St John and St Paul, he arranges for an 'orgy' (*PI* 96) to take place in their new Roman apartment. All hell breaks loose, quite literally as it even threatens Annabel's new-born baby, and everything becomes 'a shambles, an ugly mess' (*PI* 36, 52–3). In these terms, Annabel is the apotheosis of a long line of derided women who mistake neatness for veracity. Unlike the literalness of Spark's 1958 story, 'You Should Have Seen the Mess' (*CS* 155–60), Annabel's public image becomes a figurative means of tidying up reality. By shattering this image with a series of lies, Frederick's mendacious story-telling leads to the revelation of untidy truths. A continuation of Sandy Stranger and Jean Taylor, he is a necessary betrayer or good Judas figure who is rightly disloyal to false myth-makers. In a book where all the modes of plot-making are deeply flawed there is no longer an easy choice between good and evil fictions. Frederick's amoral fabrications not only expose Annabel's insidious public image but also unleash the forces of depravity – drug addicts, blackmailers and the mass media – onto her. Only a small 'pig-child' (*PI* 100), sounding uncannily like the ghost of Frederick, briefly and unequivocally speaks the truth.

Annabel's eventual bid for liberty and personal growth is a spontaneous decision, as Ruth Whittaker rightly notes, based on the 'weight' (*PI* 124) of her baby, and has little moral import.[3] As we have seen, unlike Spark's previous protagonists, Annabel lacks intelligence and so intuitively rejects the artifice of her prior existence for a more natural life. Annabel's inability to articulate this new-found awareness is significant as Spark, as we have seen, was to consistently champion intelligence over instinct. For this reason, Annabel remains merely an 'empty shell' who contains the 'echo and harking image of former and former seas' (*PI* 125). Even when viewed sympathetically, she continues to be a vacuum who needs to be filled with meaning. Only children and babies, it seems, have any intrinsic worth in this book. The love of children, not always a feature of her earlier novels, is the one form of sentiment which Spark appears to tolerate. In her next novel, *The Driver's Seat* (1970), even this emotional predilection is disallowed.

The Driver's Seat has its genesis in a macabre 1957 short story, 'The Girl I Left Behind Me' (*CS* 357–60), which recreates the consciousness of an unnamed murder victim leading up to her death. In a reversal of this earlier tale, the virtually anonymous Lise in *The Driver's Seat* leaves her life behind to actively seek out her murderer. She, too, is caught somewhere between the here and the hereafter. Although this later novella is short in length, it remains one of Spark's most accomplished works. Spark herself continues to regard it as her 'most classic novel and the most satisfactory. The construction seems to me the most complete'.[4] Written for the first time almost entirely in the present tense, with nine decisive flash-forwards, it has the classic Aristotelian virtue of taking place within a day-long period. In the minimum of space and time, Spark, with considerable technical precision, manages to include a good many of her lifelong preoccupations.

Lise resembles Annabel in being an anti-self or *tabula rasa* who is epitomized by her exteriority and lack of an inner being and, to this end, she is not even given a surname. There are elaborate descriptions of what she wears, what she does, and what her apartment looks like, but little or nothing of what she thinks or experiences. Another compulsive tidier, her flat is 'clean-lined and clear to return to after her work as if it were uninhabited' (*DS* 15) and is so organized that 'nothing need be seen, nothing need be left lying about' (*DS* 14). Rather like the novella itself, Lise's apartment is a masterpiece of concision and economy and exists as a means of circumscribing an absence. From *The Comforters* onwards, figures such as Mrs Georgina Hogg simply disappear when they are deemed only to inhabit the physical world. In *The Ballad of Peckham Rye*, Dougal Douglas encourages the workers of Peckham to absent themselves from their factory so as to discover a spiritual alternative to their workplace. This latter book, in fact, encourages a running joke about the morality or immorality of such 'absenteeism' (*BPR* 84). *The Driver's Seat* is a darker and more extreme vision of this social void and, to this extent, makes its subject Lise's obsessive need to absent herself from the world. As she merely acts out the 'fact of her presence' (*DS* 20), her character becomes nothing more than an expression of these knowingly unreal performances.

Lise combines Annabel's inauthenticity with Frederick's ability to turn his death into a fiction. As with Frederick, there are no reasons given for Lise's actions other than her need to overcome her sense of rootlessness and, as a spinster, her loneliness. In a pastiche of formulaic detective fiction, she makes elaborate arrangements for her murderer to be discovered. The carefully laid clues which she leaves behind, to help trace her movements leading to her death, finally become her story. But she, crucially, does not anticipate the sordid journalistic reconstruction of her actions which inevitably distorts her intricate plans. In Spark's previous work, the appearance of death acts as a reminder that her imaginative creations were exceeded by a sense of eternity. By the time of *The Driver's Seat*, death remains untransfigured and is turned into a second-rate story which can be sensationalized in the mass media. No longer is there a conversionist transformation of life into art or of death into truth. For Lise, the man who will eventually murder her is 'not really a presence', more 'the lack of an absence' (*DS* 71). In fact, her killer becomes an absurd parody of the convert when he laments that, before meeting Lise, he was 'hoping to start a new life' (*DS* 107). The only thing that Lise learns by manipulating her death is 'how final is finality' (*DS* 107) which is, starkly, the antithesis of any form of redemption.

Lise's materialist view of death, as nothing more than an empty dramatization, brands her as an essentially worldly myth-maker. As Jennifer Randisi has noted, Lise's deterministic role in *The Driver's Seat*, which is vindicated by its title, is that of a usurper of both God and the writer.[5] She attempts to take complete control of her own destiny – including the power over life and death – as well as the novelist's ability to turn action into plot. At one point, Lise is described as being like 'a stag scenting the breeze', searching for a 'certain air-current' (*DS* 72–3), while the book's narrator disavows any understanding of her subject, 'Who knows her thoughts? Who can tell?' (*DS* 50). Although she embodies a monomaniacal willpower, in arranging her own death, Lise also occupies the unknowable natural realm of instinct and intuition. Her attempt to rigidly control reality is thus always countered by examples of anarchic randomness and contingency – student riots, political coups, crackpot dogmatists – which she is unable to command. For this reason, her mechanical and controlled behaviour is constantly interrupted by a kind of demonic laughter as if to expose the limitations of her single-mindedness. She is quite literally 'dressed for a carnival' (*DS* 69) and when told this to her face Lise finds herself 'laughing without possibility of restraint, like a stream bound to descend whatever slope lies before it' (*DS* 69). This carnivalesque laughter, also a force of nature, acts as an essential counterpoint to her more calculated plans.

In the end, Lise's killer also rapes her so as to reveal with brutal precision her ultimate inability to order reality. After Lise's pleading that 'I don't want any sex' (*DS* 106), her murderer, in a telling slippage, 'plunges into her, with the knife poised high' (*DS* 106). What counts, as always, is Spark's precise and poetic use of language which again demonstrates the presence of a higher (albeit flawed) authority and the ridiculousness of Lise's claims to be able to determine her existence. By juxtaposing the present tense narrative with the occasional proleptic shift into the future tense, it is made clear that Lise's 'end' is not what she had envisaged. Whereas Lise fills her sense of dislocation and homelessness with a set of unreal enactments, or false conversions, her author stresses those arbitrary aspects of reality which are beyond her grasp. Lise, finally, is punished for attempting to displace her creator from the text.

In 'The Desegregation of Art', Spark defined the art of ridicule as an attempt to 'penetrate to the marrow' so as to 'paralyse its object' (DA 25). This description sounds not unlike a kind of rape which the author, in a breathtaking fictional strategy, was to inflict on her anti-heroine. Spark's intentionally heartless story substitutes any notion of rebirth with the unredeemed violence of rape and death. She also punishes, severely, the writer manqué for daring to misuse the skills of the artist. Her brutal narrator, in this way, exposes just how savage are the arts of fiction-making as well as the times at hand.

Not to Disturb (1971) is a radical extension of her previous two works as it turns death into a commodity and makes this perverted conversion her abiding theme. The novella takes place in Château Klopstock and has a time-span of only a few hours. Its main action happens off-stage and concerns an erotic triangle consisting of the Baron and Baroness von Klopstock and their personal secretary, Victor Passerat, who lock themselves in the Château's library where they are not to be disturbed. Spark focuses on a group of disparate servants who plan to profit from the foreseen deaths of the condemned threesome and who are orchestrated by Lister, the spokesman for those below stairs. In a depraved world devoid of human value, the Baron and Baroness 'haunt the house ... like insubstantial bodies, while still alive' (*ND* 23). This is a place where the dead are made substantial by becoming part of a sensational fiction which can be sold to the mass media. When deemed not to be part of the anticipated story, Spark's protagonists are dismissed as 'insubstantial bodies'.

With poetic concision, Spark's eleventh novel is her most extreme example of what has been rightly characterized as 'end-directed' or 'death-directed' fictions. Malcolm Bradbury, who has written about Spark in these terms, argues that 'endings satisfy our desire for structure and our sense of concord ... because they give to the time of the world a design of significance'.[6] Such teleological or end-directed narratives are, by definition, deterministic as their meaning is derived not from a diverse present but from an already established future. Lister, pointedly, dismisses 'vulgar chronology' (*ND* 40) as he does not want to 'split hairs...between the past, present and future tenses' (*ND* 6). By conflating past, present and future, Lister can claim that 'to all intents and purposes, [those in the library] are already dead although as a matter of banal fact, the night's business has to accomplish itself' (*ND* 12). In thinking of a life-story as part of a predetermined design, other possible futures are of necessity excluded and diminished. It is such foregone conclusions, or lack of free will, that most concerned Spark in *The Prime of Miss Jean Brodie*.

On one level, *Not to Disturb* is the infernal result of a world completely bereft of human agency. But, unlike Spark's previous work, it directs the fundamental criticism of such determinism inwards and challenges the false omniscience of the novelist. Lister is as self-assured as Jean Brodie but he has absolutely no counter-voices to challenge him. He is both a superficial impresario, coordinating the world's media, and a decidedly literary figure citing many of Spark's primary influences from the book of Job, Shakespeare and the Jacobeans, to James, Dickens and Yeats. In these terms, he is essentially a parody of his creator who was once herself determined to turn the messiness of life into a controlled and ordered narrative. Echoing Spark, in her autobiography, he wishes to 'speak of facts' as opposed to 'inconsequential talk' (*ND* 5). And, in a defining moment, he notes that 'there remain a good many things to be accomplished and still more chaos effectively to organise' (*ND* 44). The organization of chaos in *Not to Disturb* means transforming the doomed Klopstocks and Passerat into a marketable fiction. As with the anti-selves in Spark's previous two books, Lister ensures, above all else, that life must be subordinated to an essentially unredemptive art. In a chilling commentary on the misguided primacy of the writer, the lives of those in the library are sacrificed so as to provide material for a money-spinning story.

Not to Disturb has rightly been described as a work of 'consummate fictiveness'.[7] Everything in this short novel is artificial and theatrical from its programmatic temporal and spatial Aristotelian virtues to its five chapters (corresponding to five acts), its many allusions to Jacobean drama, and its remarkable range of mainly Victorian literary clichés. These include a gothic dark and stormy night, a lunatic in the attic, a haunted house, a couple begging for admission, and the mysterious deaths in the library. The Klopstocks' Château turns out to be only eleven years old and is, like the novel itself, a contemporary pastiche of different styles and traditions.

Spark's familiar eternal triangle is also based on entrenched sexual conventions, with its protagonists merely acting out a series of erotic impersonations. Theo the chauffeur, detached from the main action, rightly observes that the reason for the mutual hostility between Cathy and Cecil Klopstock is that she has stopped 'playing the game' (*ND* 35) and has decided to 'go natural' (*ND* 35) by refusing her enforced role-play. But even this supposedly plausible summary is, ironically, just another disingenuous game as it turns out to be the plot of *The Public Image*. Everyone becomes subordinated to the force of Lister's narrative whether they be clergymen, the police, visiting aristocracy, or Baron Klopstock's deranged younger brother. Even the couple wandering the grounds of the Château are eventually killed off by a stroke of lightning as 'they do not come into the story' (*ND* 31). Spark's marshalling of the art of story-telling, not unlike Lister's, is carried out with military precision.

Ultimately, both the form and content of *Not to Disturb* are transformed into a dangerous artifice which fatally confuses life and art. It is the reduction of the world to an already known fiction which enables Lister to say that the Klopstocks have 'placed themselves ... within the realm of predestination' (*ND* 37). The supposedly Swiss Klopstocks sound suspiciously alien – not unlike the Kleins or Klipsteins in the poetry of T. S. Eliot – which seems to signal that their foreignness needs to be contained by a higher order. In similar fashion, the household servants are also a cosmopolitan amalgam made up of several different languages and nationalities in search of a fallacious (because monetary) 'harmony' (*ND* 21). This unreal and fabricated world, in other words, conforms to Spark's own sense of racial and national dislocation before her conversion. But, in a key reversal, it is no longer possible to emulate Spark and to transcend a displaced cosmopolitan identity by entering a unifying story. On the contrary, *Not to Disturb* is suspicious of the very processes of aesthetic transfiguration which are at the heart of both fiction-making and the act of conversion. The relationship of art to the world is now a form of negative redemption which turns the dead, in a cruel mutation, into mundane clichés.

Alan Bold has maintained that Spark, in this work, is challenging the determinism of the novel form with a more poetic anti-determinist mode of fiction.[8] But there is very little evidence for this argument. On the contrary, most of Lister's pronouncements, as we have seen, mimic Spark's own beliefs. His narrative is not only inauthentically materialistic, as its only purpose is financial gain, but it is also authentically literary, citing many of the writers at the heart of the Western canon. Where Spark does distinguish herself absolutely from Lister is in the separation of art from life. When asked by Heloise whether the Klopstocks will feel 'anything' (*ND* 45) when they die, Lister replies, echoing Yeats, 'does a flame feel pain?' (*ND* 45). But his reference to Yeats's 'Sailing to Byzantium' transforms the Klopstocks into a metaphor and confirms Yeats's own misgivings at creating an imaginary homeland which supplants his own ailing body.

Lister's aesthetic dehumanization of the Klopstocks illustrates the profound dangers of transmuting reality into words. On one level, everything is distorted, deformed and misshapen in this work, whether it be through McGuire's tape-recorder or Samuel's camera or the many one-eyed versions of the Klopstock debacle that abound. But these mechanical processes of shaping and editing are, however inauthentic, also akin to the literary arts. Poetry cannot, as Bold assumes, be easily placed outside of these aesthetic choices. With brutal honesty, Spark does associate her desire to mythologize the world, and redeem a dead self, with Lister's inhuman narrative. Her brilliantly concise novella wisely questions the need to convert life into art and the savage materialism which is at the core of this creative act. All acts of the imagination, according to this work, are bound by their very nature to falsify reality. For this reason, Spark no longer allows the reader to make easy distinctions between good and evil stories. For the writer, in this dark mood, everything is reduced to complete absurdity.

All three of these secular parables expose the amoral will of the individual in determining reality, which mimics Spark's own practices as a novelist. In a telling departure from her previous work, Spark acts as if the transfiguration of the commonplace is no longer possible and, in a calculated reversal, she leaves her fiction radically unconverted and machine-like. Rather like Dougal Douglas before them, Spark's dubious fictionalizers – such as Frederick Christopher, Lise and Lister – are all horrendously plausible. As well as highlighting an irredeemably absurd humanity, Spark is also showing the folly of all those, including herself, who wish to transfigure the world. In a move that will lead to a more complete form of anarchy in her subsequent work, Spark has rejected a god-like narrative authority for the more devilish arts of ridicule. These three outstanding novellas mark a moment of absolute transition in Spark's output. With devastating effect, they all expose the simple-mindedness of the religious and formalistic ordering principles which had hitherto sustained her. By demonstrating so clearly the falsifying power of art, she has, paradoxically, created a sense of what is missing from her fictions – that is, the truth. In her next four books, as we will now see, Spark was to locate her sense of absurdity and sceptical authority at the very heart of her truth-giving philosophy.

6

International Messes: Between Life and Art

Muriel Spark's next four books – *The Hothouse by the East River* (1973), *The Abbess of Crewe* (1974), *The Takeover* (1976) and *Territorial Rights* (1979) – all gradually move away from the classically concise literary form of her previous three novels. After these coldly impersonal works, Spark was to relinquish her illusion of god-like narrative control and the minimalism which allowed her to command every aspect of her foreshortened universe. But her renunciation of authorial mastery is no longer in deference to a higher transcendental truth but due to the riotous and unrestrained nature of contemporary reality. In this phase of her writing, encompassing most of the 1970s, Spark alludes either explicitly or implicitly to the Cold War, the Watergate scandal (1972–4), the Middle Eastern oil crisis (1973–4), the rise of political kidnapping and international terrorism and, more generally, to the ever-changing vicissitudes of global capitalism. This is a world which has spun out of control and which is terminally in crisis. No wonder Spark is unable to construct a narrative, however flawed, to contain such turmoil.

Spark's all-encompassing sense of danger and uncertainty is reflected in her eventual return to the heterodox and anarchic literary form of *The Mandelbaum Gate* (which was, in turn, designed to mirror Middle Eastern discord). In *The Mandelbaum Gate*, Spark's maverick community of exiles – the potentially insane or sexually and politically perverse – included a characteristically arch-category known as 'international messes' (*MG* 101). Much of Spark's subsequent fiction, culminating in *The Takeover* and *Territorial Rights*, can be described as 'international messes'. No longer able to turn reality into a coherent story-line, Spark has begun to relish the worldly confusions which she had hitherto transfigured in her fiction. At the beginning of her career, Spark attempted to distinguish rigorously between those who are life-giving truth-tellers and those who are death-inducing mythomaniacs. By the 1970s, however, Spark is able to accept her outrageous mythologizers as figures who embody a material world which itself cannot tell the difference between truth and artistry. Spark's religious and aesthetic ordering principles had previously enabled her to make sense of a meaningless universe. But, by the time of *The Hothouse by the East River*, Spark had given up on such overly simple ways of portraying reality. From now on, she would embrace the chaos that surrounded her and not merely attempt to banish it to a lesser domain.

The Hothouse by the East River has a peculiar place in Spark's oeuvre. Although published in 1973, two years after *Not to Disturb*, it was begun initially in 1965 just as she was finishing *The Mandelbaum Gate*.[1] For this reason, the novel is a transition text which incorporates the autobiographical concerns of Spark's earlier fiction but locates them in the impersonal and 'externalized' (*HER* 46) realm of her more recent work. Set in contemporary New York, as Spark lived in this city in the early 1960s, *The Hothouse by the East River* is split between past and present, Europe and the United States, and truth and absurdity. In short, two different versions of Spark's fictional agenda clash in this work. On the one hand, the novel is written in the present tense, like all of her most recent books, and continues to be fascinated by a senseless world of inversions. At the same time her heroine, Elsa Hazlett, is reminiscent of her earlier truth-telling personae who are able to discern an underlying morality beneath the corrupt surface. New York is thus a place of irrationality *par excellence* which is rationalized as such by Spark's representative voice. Here there is a softening of tone as the power of her later works is precisely that everyone captured within their ambit is utterly consumed by the absurdity that surrounds them.

In thematic terms, much of *The Hothouse by the East River* is a significant continuation of the key motifs of *The Public Image* and *Not to Disturb*. It begins with the phrase, 'If it were only true that all's well that ends well, if it were only true' (*HER* 5), as if to question her previous obsession with endings in her work. At the same time, it refers back to Spark's earlier ghost stories, such as 'The Portobello Road' (1958), where death is no longer a point of closure. *The Hothouse by the East River* takes this preoccupation a stage further by peopling 1970s New York with ghosts who have refused to succumb to the particular ending designed for them. It turns out that Paul and Elsa Hazlett, who had planned to emigrate to the United States after the war, were both killed in 1944 when a V-2 bomb fell directly on the train in which they were travelling. Paul Hazlett, however, rejects his fate and his ensuing restlessness causes him to invent an illusory future for himself and his wife. The novel is, in this way, conflicted between Paul's seductive unreality and the harsh realities of the past which eventually overwhelm him. His all-consuming desire to create a destiny which has not been predetermined is akin to the novelist's self-deluding need to redeem the world through a capricious imagination. As with much of her later work, Spark's fiction is in tension with this redemptive impulse and is haunted by a past which refuses to be contained.

Much of the black comedy in *The Hothouse by the East River* derives from the fact that the apparitions within it are more vibrant and alive than are contemporary New Yorkers. Paul 'can't tell the difference' (*HER* 134) between the living and the dead in Manhattan although he thinks, crucially, that 'one should live first, then die, not die then live; everything in its own time' (*HER* 119). Spark ironically evokes a sense of eternity only to have her ghostly figures reduce it to more manageable temporal proportions. There is a deliberately farcical restoration of order which results in Elsa, for instance, viewing her 'deadly body...in full health, dusting the dust away' (*HER* 96). Much less comical is the perception of the living as if they were already dead. New York is pointedly described as the 'home of the vivisectors of the mind . . . and home of those whose minds have been dead, bearing scars of resurrection' (*HER* 11). It is the living, in other words, who have been brought back from the dead as opposed to the dead who are in 'full health'. In a particularly horrifying scene, Princess Xavier accidentally hatches the eggs of silk-worms on her breasts and thus becomes a rotting corpse while still alive. Such reversals characterize this work, which contains, most tellingly, a grotesque version of J. M. Barrie's *Peter Pan* played by a wholly geriatric cast.

Paul, rather like Frederick Christopher in *The Public Image*, has an obsessive need to mythologize his death and turn it into a decidedly troubled form of fiction-making. On the one hand, his unreal New York continues to 'haunt' (*HER* 88) him just as he is haunted by his past. Not unlike Spark's other arch male rationalists, he is unable to comprehend the supernatural and considers everyone around him, Elsa included, to be insane. He is, especially, unable to cope with Elsa's mysteriously inverted shadow which he regards as 'a mirage...Not a fact' (*HER* 8). At the same time, it is his extreme jealousy of Helmut Kiel that has driven him to invent a new life in the first place. Helmut, a German prisoner of war, also died in 1944 and was the source of much erotic commotion between Paul and Elsa. Their war-time history, working for a 'black propaganda' (*HER* 52) organization, draws directly on Spark's own life-story. As she was to recount in *Curriculum Vitae: A Volume of Autobiography* (1992), Spark helped broadcast allied propaganda during the Second World War in the form of a plausible German news programme. Her experience of disseminating often grotesque lies in the guise of the truth was, in retrospect, a perfect training for her absurdist fictions.

When Elsa sees Helmut again in a New York shoe shop, Paul's unbounded emotions run rampant and speak from the grave: '"Help me! Help me!" cries his heart, battering the sides of the coffin. "The schizophrenic has imposed her will. Her delusion, her figment, her nothing-there has come to pass"' (*HER* 15). Later on, Elsa accuses Paul's 'imagination' of 'running away with itself' (*HER* 126) as he has begun to believe utterly in his bogus existence. But, unlike Spark's preceding mythomaniacs, Paul's neurotic projections are meant to be an apt commentary on an absurd world. Part of the novel's confusion is that Paul's sense of absurdity is neatly resolved by Elsa's spiritual certainties. Thus, New York's heat wave becomes a form of purgatory with Elsa's inverted shadow – combining Dante's Purgatorio with Peter Pan – signifying both Barrie's Never-Never Land and a divine order of knowledge. By the end, Elsa trails her 'faithful and lithe cloud of unknowing across the pavement' (*HER* 140), gaining spiritual weight from the anonymous fourteenth-century mystic who wrote *The Cloud of Unknowing*. But this conclusion merely highlights the uneasy tension between Paul's amoral ghost-story, with the living wholly lacking substance, and Elsa's transcendent satire, with the universe restored to its rightful moral order. After this book, Paul's inversion of reason and unreason, fact and fantasy, will correspond exactly with Spark's own sense of a chaotic and irredeemable reality.

Spark's next novel, *The Abbess of Crewe* (1974), is a much less confused work which directs its satire inwards so as to address acutely the foundations of her most basic assumptions. In contrast to *The Hothouse by the East River*, Spark makes absurd her most dearly held beliefs and thereby refuses a too easy space outside of the text where all can be clarified. The eponymous heroine of this beguiling and witty novel is a combination of Miss Jean Brodie and Lister in her arrogant vivacity and egomaniacal plot-making. Another of Spark's novelists manqués, Alexandra, the would-be Lady Abbess, is a knowing myth-maker who, from the beginning, tells her confidantes that she is 'your conscience and your authority' (*AC* 8). Like Lister, and the omniscient Sparkian narrator of old, she parodies the deity in the book of Genesis who looks upon her convent 'as if upon a certain newly created world' and 'sees it is good' (*AC* 28). As with all of Spark's wilful determiners of reality, her 'destiny' (*AC* 32), to be elected the Abbess of Crewe, constrains all those within her purview. But, in stark contrast to Jean Brodie, there is very little overt criticism of Alexandra who, if a diabolical figure as some readers have argued, is absolved from authorial criticism and is completely endorsed by the book's narrator.

What is most startling about Alexandra is that, although an outrageous figure, she is Spark's most complete and sympathetic fictional double. Alexandra is the apotheosis of the 'different-from' Catholic who is given complete licence to castigate her 'same as' subordinates. For this reason, she shows complete disdain for the ordinary nuns in the convent: 'A less edifying crowd of human life it would be difficult to find . . .' (*AC* 50). As with the Marcia Blaine School or the May of Teck Club, Spark is at pains to debunk facile expectations concerning the virtuous disposition of a community of young women. But, unlike her previous books, it is not a false innocence that Spark is most keen to satirize but the sheer lack of 'individualism' (*AC* 61) which can result from these homogenizing communities. Alexandra, in other words, has the same role in relation to her convent as the novelist has in relation to society as a whole. As with her author, she ridicules imperiously a world which has destroyed the individual spirit. Although an arch-mythologizer and determinist, Alexandra is forgiven absolutely everything because she is able to vitalize a humdrum reality in much the same way as Spark herself.

Unlike her previous books, where the novelist's arts are treated with suspicion, if not downright disdain, *The Abbess of Crewe* is a paean of praise to these manipulative skills. Throughout the novel, Alexandra is characterized by her beauty which results in her being described as an 'object of art...the end of which is to give pleasure' (*AC* 105). She is absolutely clear about the need for her to 'perform her part in the drama of *The Abbess of Crewe*' (*AC* 24) and there are many examples of her flamboyant presence dazzling large audiences. Such performances are wonderfully instrumental and are described by her as 'entertaining scenarios' (*AC* 89) which cynically obfuscate the truth. She describes such scenarios as 'an art-form...based on facts. A good scenario is a garble. A bad one is a bungle. They need not be plausible, only hypnotic, like all good art' (*AC* 89). Alexandra is an 'object of art' precisely because she has a 'hypnotic' hold over all who encounter her (not least her readers). Her artistry, in other words, is able to transform and humanize those around her. Spark gives her many set piece scenes, or scenarios, to demonstrate fully the marvellous effect of her enchanting stratagems.

In the opening chapter of the novel, Alexandra argues that 'the ages of the Father and the Son are past. We have entered the age of the Holy Ghost', and goes on to claim that 'I move as the Spirit moves me' (*AC* 10). Later on, she argues that 'to each her own source of grace' (*AC* 82). There is a strong sense in which Alexandra's graceful artistry is related to this spiritual age which complements the corporeality of the Father and Son. Both the Abbess's aesthetic power and her feminine grace are associated with the Holy Ghost and are seen to disrupt the masculine sameness of the Catholic Church. This aspect of the novel is explored more fully in Spark's next book, *The Takeover* and has been a preoccupation of hers since *Robinson*. It is not a coincidence that Spark herself speaks of the Holy Ghost as 'her favourite person of the Trinity'.[2] Both fiction and femininity, it seems, are subversive of male power in whatever form it might take.

Along with the timeless Holy Spirit, Alexandra's story has a profane temporal dimension which Spark is also keen to heighten. One oversimplified reading of this book is to see Alexandra's quest for power as an allegory of the Watergate affair – an ongoing scandal which was taking place during the book's composition – which culminated in the impeachment of the American president, Richard Nixon. In these terms, Alexandra is a Nixonian figure who masterminds burglaries, rigs elections, electronically bugs her rival, Sister Felicity, and covers up her activities when discovered. Alexandra, like Nixon, has two close confidantes, Sister Mildred and Sister Warburga (akin to John Ehrlichman and Bob Haldeman), and her globe-trotting and deep-voiced counsel, Sister Gertrude, sounds unmistakably like Nixon's Secretary of State, Henry Kissinger. Spark plays with these parallels throughout the novel, as Alan Bold has shown in detail, but it would be a mistake to reduce the book to an uncomplicated satire of worldly corruption.[3]

What is most notable about Alexandra is that her glorious presence is able to bestride both the spiritual and material domains. She declares that 'here, in the Abbey of Crewe, we have discarded history. We have entered the sphere...of mythology....Who doesn't yearn to be part of a myth at whatever price of comfort?' (AC 16). For her, 'mythology is nothing more than history garbled; likewise history is mythology garbled' (AC 87). As 'good art' is, essentially, a 'garble' (AC 89) – a lie leading to the truth – Alexandra mythologizes herself so as to contain all of these oppositions. She is, in this way, a unifier par excellence who brings together the disparate spheres of history and mythology, politics and art, the temporal and the spiritual. The novel is consequently full of juxtaposed realms such as liturgy and literature, theology and technology, and reads somewhat like a farcical prayer. Just as Spark, in her abiding quest for wholeness, wished to 'desegregate' reality in theory, Alexandra is seen to do it in practice. Alexandra and her author engage in an aesthetic, as opposed to a merely religious, ordering of the world.

So as to redeem her from the demonic potential of her artistry, Alexandra's capricious rule is, most importantly, always formally limited by the convent's regular acts of devotion (which constantly interrupt her Machiavellian schemes to win the election). Spark extends her sympathy to Alexandra precisely because she is able to encompass the tension between the secular and the divine. What is more, when placed next to Sister Felicity's extreme worldliness and Sister Gertrude's complete detachment from the material life of the convent, Alexandra is seen to have a more balanced view of reality. Here there is a key distinction to be made between Alexandra and her prototype, Jean Brodie. In *The Prime of Miss Jean Brodie*, the omniscient authorial voice argues that Jean Brodie was 'by temperament suited only to the Roman Catholic Church' which might have 'embraced, even while it disciplined, her soaring and diving spirit' (*PMJB* 85). Without such discipline Brodie is, quite literally, allowed to run riot. Alexandra's 'soaring and diving spirit', on the other hand, is constrained by her Catholicism which utilizes the anarchy of artistic creation to disturb the sobriety of a higher faith.

Compared to her previous work, *The Abbess of Crewe* is an optimistic endorsement of Spark's initial faith that life can be converted into art and that this albeit partial transfiguration may lead to a lasting truth. Sister Gertrude, in a more restricted way, attempts to convert 'cannibals' in Africa with 'dietary concessions and the excessive zeal of vegetarian heretics suppressed' (*AC* 42). In a devastating critique of Gertrude's Catholic orthodoxies, which aim merely to convert those in Africa, Alexandra argues that 'It seems to me, Gertrude ... that your shoulds and shouldn'ts have been established rather nearer home, let us say the continent of Europe, if you will forgive the expression' (*AC* 91). Through her artistry and force of personality, Alexandra, in stark contrast to Gertrude, attempts to convert those nearer home whom she suspects of suffering from 'universal dementia' (*AC* 54). To this extent, far from being a diabolical figure, she is the uneasy exemplar of Spark's aesthetic ideals.

As she sets sail for Rome to prove her innocence, Alexandra asks that all references to poetry be deleted from her copious surveillance tapes. Her argument is that the verses which she has uttered are 'proper to myself alone and should not be cast before the public' (*AC* 106). Here the essential privacy and ambiguity of art, a unifier merely of a corrupt humanity, is placed in its proper perspective. With *The Takeover*, Spark extends her critique of Roman Catholicism to the national sphere by setting her book in a specifically Italian social and political context (in her previous work Italy tended to be merely a passive backdrop). In this novel, art is no longer reduced to the private realm but invades every aspect of public life. The aestheticizing power of Alexandra has, seemingly, been extended from the Abbey of Crewe to the heart of Catholic influence and power. Spark herself, in 1966, was to move to Rome and has subsequently lived mainly in Italy. The journey to her spiritual heartland, not unlike Alexandra's parallel excursion, was accompanied by a publicly sceptical attitude towards the institutions of the Catholic Church.[4] Once based in Italy, Spark was able to make absurd an organized religion that was now part of her everyday life.

By the time of *The Takeover*, set between 1973 and 1975, Italy has ceased to be a place of Catholic authority and is, instead, an essentially disruptive locale which she thinks of as a real-life comic opera. At one point, Spark's narrator describes the Watergate scandal as releasing 'everyone's latent anarchism' (*T* 54) which we have already seen personified in the guise of the Nixonian rebel, Alexandra. One main reason for this sense of disorder, caused by the Watergate affair, is that it exposes the falsity of patriarchal rule, a central feature of *The Takeover*. Critics have rightly related this book to *The Mandelbaum Gate* in terms of its length, unrestrained narrative form, ambitious historical reach, and its reversion to the past tense. Some commentators have even dubbed *The Takeover* her 'most anarchic novel', a label previously applied to *The Mandelbaum Gate*.[5] In the earlier work, the confrontation with 'the System' (*MG* 81), essentially father-figures of all kinds (including the Pope), tended to be restricted to a marginalized group of national and sexual deviants who, on the cusp of madness and prophecy, have a curiously ambivalent place in the book. With *The Takeover*, however, a sweeping critique of the economic and political system, especially the capitalist West, pervades the novel as a whole and goes beyond the manic influence of these small groupings.

In a key intervention, we are told with complete narrative approval that during the last quarter of 1973, dubbed without irony 'the Dark Ages II' (*T* 99), there had been the 'beginning of something new in the world; a change in the meaning of money and property' (*T* 90). Although the book's title refers to financial takeovers of all kinds, it also denotes a sense of the 'takeover' of a particular era by a wholly other set of values. Spark, in one edition, subtitled her novel 'A Parable of the Pagan Seventies'[6] and her wealthy characters speak of

> the mood of the stock-market, the health of the economy as if these were living creatures with moods and blood. And thus they personalized and demonologized the abstractions of their lives, believing them to be fundamentally real, indeed changeless. But it did not occur to one of those spirited and in various ways intelligent people ... that a complete mutation of our means of nourishment had already come into being ... a complete mutation not merely to be defined as the collapse of the capitalist system, or a global recession, but such a sea-change in the nature of reality as could not have been envisaged by Karl Marx or Sigmund Freud. (*T* 90–1)

Crucially, Spark dates this 'sea-change' to the October 1973 'battle in the Middle East' (*T* 91) and she thus associates the origins of this apocalyptic shift with the Arab–Israeli war and the subsequent 'oil trauma' (*T* 99). Echoing *The Mandelbaum Gate*, the Middle East once again becomes the source of all chaos, in particular the confusion of materiality and spirituality. In this dangerous new world, 'assets' become 'liabilities' (*T* 91) and, as with *The Hothouse by the East River*, 'appearances are reality' (*T* 72). History has, in the words of the Abbess of Crewe, entered the 'sphere of mythology' (*AC* 16). Maggie Radcliffe, Spark's reluctant heroine, is swindled out of her fortune by a plausible impostor, which is a result of her being taken in by these overwhelming fabrications. In a world without meaning, Hubert Mallindaine, Maggie's unwitting redeemer, is able to illegally occupy with impunity one of her three villas on Lake Nemi.

Much of the plot revolves around the eventual unification of Maggie's unthinking materialism with Hubert's 'avid immaterialism' (*T* 106) which, when separated, are equally symptomatic of a new Dark Age. Hubert, Spark's maverick anti-hero, makes out a compelling case for the contemporary world as a form of 'semblance' (*T* 72) and, essentially, as part of the aesthetic realm. For this reason, *The Takeover* is chock full of fakes and disguises of all kinds which Hubert is able to take complete advantage of. Because of the sea-change in reality, nothing is what it seems and everything has a surface value which, when explored further, is shown to be worthless. In these terms, Hubert is not unlike a Sparkian interpreter of his author's fiction: 'Reality is subjective...I say that even [the Catholic] religion is based on individual perception of appearances only. Apart from these, there is no reality' (*T* 73). Hubert describes himself as a 'mystic' (*T* 73) and has a 'laughter demon' (*T* 15) which, like his author, subverts all forms of authority whether they be financial, religious or philosophical. Thus, he has a splendid disregard for the wealth which surrounds him, goes back to the pagan or magical roots of Catholicism, and regards 'literal truth' (*T* 98) as a form of 'gross materialism' (*T* 99):

> The concepts of property and material possession are the direct causes of such concepts as perjury, lying, deception and fraud. In the world of symbol and the worlds of magic, of allegory and mysticism, deceit has no meaning, lies do not exist, fraud is impossible. These concepts are impossible because the materialist standards of conduct from which they arise are non-existent. (*T* 99)

These words could quite easily have been uttered by Alexandra who, like Hubert, is an arch-mythologizer of reality who discounts a materialist standard of conduct. For her as well, everything is a semblance and there is no such thing as earthly truths. Spark's critics have mistakenly dismissed Hubert (along with Alexandra) as a wicked spirit whose egomania is symptomatic of his false faith. The assumption of these moralizing readings is that Hubert's paganism and worship of Diana and Apollo is in a long line of unchristian demonic figures beginning with the occultist, Baron Stock, in *The Comforters* and the spiritualist, Patrick Seton, in *The Bachelors*.[7] To be sure, Hubert's homosexuality and rampant immaterialism does relate him, in part, to the fraudulent world of Patrick Seton ('Satan') in *The Bachelors*. What is more, the murderous Seton, in this earlier work, is pointedly described as being 'like a Christian convert of the jungle who secretly returns by night to the fetish tree' (*B* 145) (or an originary paganism). But, as soon as this comparison is made, it is clear how far Spark has moved from this erstwhile moralistic text. Hubert, not unlike her more recent protagonists, is a decidedly ambivalent figure who offers a welcome alternative to a predominant materialism. Instead of thinking of Spark's work as a continuous whole, organized around the same moral typology, it is worth noting the manner in which her preoccupations have changed radically over time.

Both *The Bachelors* and *The Takeover* refer back to Spark's essay on Marcel Proust and his 'sacramental vision of the world' (RA 1). Spark does not merely condemn Hubert for lacking a 'sacramental vision' (as her characters were condemned in *The Bachelors*), but instead draws on her cunning appropriation of Proust as a 'deeply religious writer' who happened to have a 'pagan aesthetic':

> Lacking a redemptive faith, Proust's attempt was to save himself through art. And in refreshing our vision from a writer like Proust, we are following the tradition whereby a great amount of the most fruitful thought of the Church is derived from the efforts of inspired pagans to save themselves. (*RA* 1)

Hubert, like Proust, is a homosexual (Spark describes Proust as a 'sexual pervert') and he is, above all else, an 'inspired pagan'. What is more, not unlike Spark's version of Proust, he attempts to reintroduce the source of all magic into the Church. Hubert, significantly, reverses J. G. Frazer's influential *The Golden Bough* (1890–1915), a key reference point in the novel, which promotes a liberal view of Western civilization as moving from the pagan to the Christian era and, finally, to the scientific age. In a perverted reading of *The Golden Bough*, Hubert occupies Maggie's villa on Lake Nemi not on rational grounds but because Frazer locates the worship of the goddess Diana on the shores of the Nemi. Hubert claims to be the descendant of an illicit union between the 'Benevolent-Malign Diana of the woods' (*T* 43) and the Emperor Caligula. His mixed surname, Mallindaine, stands for 'malign Diana' but it may also be a happy coincidence that it seems to reverse Proust's resonant 'madeleine'. If the 'taste and smell' of the madeleine, in Proust's epic novel, bears 'the vast structure of recollection', then Hubert merely fabricates his supposed ancestral memories.[8] Lacking the sacramental vision of Proust, as Spark would have it (with the madeleine acting as a kind of pagan communion), Hubert is the last in a long line of Spark's unreal romantic hybrids who go back as far as the black–white Samuel Cramer in 'The Seraph and the Zambesi' (1951).

Throughout her work, beginning with the 'half gipsy' (*C* 12) Louisa Jebb in *The Comforters* and January Marlow in *Robinson*, Spark has created unifying women who offer an alternative vision to an overly rigid sense of Catholic orthodoxy. January, we remember, practises pagan ceremonies in *Robinson* as the 'pagan mind runs strong in women' (*R* 8) and anticipates the part pagan, part Judaic rituals concerning the New Moon in 'The Gentile Jewesses'. In these terms, first articulated at length in *Robinson*, the Catholic Church has become overly materialistic or masculinized and needs, above all, feminine grace. In *Robinson* it is Mariology that provides this alternative vision although the cult of the Virgin Mary is pointedly criticized by Robinson and Ian Brodie as a form of idolatry which supposedly contains 'dangerous impurities' (*R* 79) and encourages the worship of a 'pagan goddess' (*R* 78). Hubert, in *The Takeover*, takes this heterodox spiritual practice to an extreme and explicitly associates Diana worship with the 'image' of 'Mary the Mother of God' (*T* 99). In these terms, and here there is a stark contrast with the homophobia of *The Bachelors*, Hubert's homosexuality enables him, like Proust, to bring together the feminine and masculine realms of existence.

The Takeover, in this reading, is primarily about a return to origins both in terms of Spark's subject matter and of her formative preoccupations. Not that Hubert's paganism is accepted uncritically as a source of contemporary renewal. Spark makes it clear that his extreme version of paganism is ultimately riotous, and leads, finally, to a mass drug-induced orgy (*T* 156–66) and to a world of pure anarchy. On the other hand, she has great fun satirizing the Jesuit priests who visit Hubert (a favourite target lambasted in *The Abbess of Crewe*), who are merely 'doing studies of ecological paganism' (*T* 11) and rely on 'documentational listings' (*T* 75). If Hubert turns paganism into farce, then the Jesuits turn it into a purely cerebral matter. Maggie Radcliffe's reversion to the status of a moon-lit 'gipsy' (*T* 188), at the end of the novel, proves to be the perfect balance between these two extremes of spirituality and materialism. Not unlike Annabel Christopher in *The Public Image* or Cathy Klopstock in *Not to Disturb*, Maggie attempts to return to an originary state of nature in reaction to the absolute fakery of modern life. She alone recognizes the true character of those around her by responding to them in their own terms, 'Why shouldn't I be a criminal? Everyone else is' (*T* 175).

Michael Wood has understandably balked at Maggie's perverse response to the vicissitudes of global capitalism. After all, how can 'dressing like a gipsy' be, in any way, a sane rejoinder to economic danger, especially when Maggie has lost and gained a small fortune, flirted with assassination and kidnapping, and finally discovered that she no longer owns her three villas on Lake Nemi.[9] But Wood, perhaps, underestimates the extent to which Spark's gypsy-like heroines, endowed with an acute understanding of the world, have always stood as an absolute counterpoint to a prevailing religious, economic and philosophical materialism. Maggie begins the novel with a wayward spiritual belief in the 'higher market-place communion that exists between rich and rich' (*T* 29) and ends it by adopting some, although by no means all, of Hubert's atavistic practices. She therefore combines an abiding worldliness with a radically new source of redemption. Her eventual unholy alliance with her predatory servant Lauro contrasts starkly with *Not to Disturb* and indicates that she is, above all else, a unifier of opposites.

In this regard, one need only compare Maggie with Pauline Thin, Hubert's narrowly orthodox Catholic secretary (as her name suggests) who segregates reality into separate spheres. Pauline is characterized, not unlike Spark's invariably neurotic anti-heroines, as 'having an epistolary style which denotes an hysterical need for stability and order' (*T* 59). What is more, she mistakenly works in the dogmatic 'spirit of the missionaries of old who held that conversion was only a matter of revealing the true doctrine' (*T* 22). To this end, she unwittingly causes a riot by reciting from the Acts of the Apostles, during an act of Diana worship, as if this will mechanically redeem Hubert's pagan followers. When Hubert dismisses Pauline as looking like 'the commandant of a concentration camp' (*T* 153), it is clear, after the Eichmann trial, where a belief in 'the true doctrine' might lead. Far from being akin to Caroline Rose, as Ruth Whittaker argues, Pauline is not unlike the brutally doctrinaire and humourless Georgina Hogg.[10] Such is the extent to which Spark's Catholic orthodoxies are marginalized in this book.

The Takeover and her next novel, *Territorial Rights*, can be paired as unbounded full-length works whose Italian setting and amoral plot-lines mark a complete departure from the 'stability and order' and 'true doctrine' of her earlier books. At the end of *Territorial Rights*, Grace Gregory (the secular embodiment of feminine grace) captures the absurdity of Spark's fifteenth work of fiction when she wonders 'why the Roman Catholic church doesn't stick to politics and keep its nose out of morals' (*TR* 236). Set in contemporary Venice, Italy is deemed by Grace, again sounding like an interpreter of her own narrative, to be a place where the 'far-fetched' is actually a form of 'stark realism' (*TR* 161). This 'far-fetched' world, invariably loveless and treacherous, is over-determined by references to global politics of the left and the right and is made up of international spies, adulterers, murderers, blackmailers, dissenters, kidnappers and terrorists. In a self-consciously convoluted plot, which indicates its knowing fictiveness, a group of rootless cosmopolitans descend on Venice and are found to be linked both to Robert Leaver, a 24-year-old student from Birmingham, and a corpse buried during the Second World War.

By locating her story in Venice, Spark draws on a long literary tradition which portrays the city as the decaying heart of European civilization. In these terms, Venice is always in flux as it mixes old and new, East and West, which signifies both its vitality and its corruption.[11] In this 'international mess' *par excellence*, Spark pointedly makes each of her dramatis personae nomadic figures who lack 'territorial rights'. Her novel is thus, on the one hand, a diasporic global village made up of dissenting Bulgarian communists, or deracinated Americans or Britons, or Italian Jews, each of whom is at home in their homelessness. What is more, she invents international organizations such as GESS (Global-Equip Security Services) or, as in *The Takeover*, focuses on extraterritorial forces such as global capitalism and communism, international terrorism and fascist gangsterism, as specious but effective determiners of individual lives. But, whereas Hubert and Maggie are able to adapt to these powerful but essentially hollow forces, everyone in *Territorial Rights* becomes enraptured by them. This mass hysteria reaches its climax when Robert, originally a male prostitute in Paris, fakes his own kidnapping and endeavours to blackmail all those with whom he comes into contact. His fascination with violence, and excitement of all kinds, results in his being 'sent to the Middle East to train in a terrorist camp' (*TR* 238) which, in the by now familiar inversion, turns the site of the Bible into the source of disorder for the West.

Without an exceptional figure, such as Maggie Radcliffe, the novel takes to an extreme a world made up of dispossessed individuals whose gypsy-like cosmopolitanism is on the side of madness rather than unity. In this bleak vision of total pandemonium, all of the book's central characters are determined by a false universalism – the brutal global forces of an empty modernity – which crushes their humanity. *Territorial Rights*, in this regard, is not unlike Spark's previous accounts of rootless individuals who attempt to remedy their alienation from the world by mythologizing it (which is the leitmotif of much of her fiction from the 1970s onwards). At the same time, in a telling counterpoint to the power of present-day phenomena, *Territorial Rights* evokes a macabre sense of what is hidden or unexpressed as a means of compelling her characters to disengage from a ubiquitous materialism.

In this regard, the body of Victor Pancev, a Bulgarian double agent during the Second World War, becomes in effect the ghostly protagonist of *Territorial Rights*. Two sisters, Eufemia and Katerina, who own the Pensione Sofia, were both madly in love with Victor and, out of sheer jealousy, arrange for his body to be cut in two, from the head down, so as to establish 'territorial rights' over it. His body is duly buried on each side of the well-kept garden of the Pensione Sofia, with many of the novel's characters becoming heedlessly drawn into this bizarre setting. Gabriel Josipovici has rightly argued that a good deal of the book's action hinges on the body's presence even though it is never uncovered.[12] In this reading, the body represents a wholly other set of values to the empty materialism of Venice. As the apprentice who helped the 'fascist butcher' (*TR* 149) dispose of Victor during the war puts it: 'they have the body in the garden, sliced in two. That's concrete. Everything else is anything else you like' (*TR* 218). Once again, it is the dead who convey the truth, the happenings of the living are insubstantial. With typical Sparkian wit, Violet remarks that 'there is the question of the body…The rest is immaterial' (*TR* 143).

The novel revolves around a weird set-piece scene which finds

Victor's daughter, the outrageously anti-Semitic Lina Pancev, unwittingly dancing on her father's grave. This stark image of desecration is placed uneasily next to the assumption of an underlying plenitude or truth. In these terms, a sense of an alternative perspective – which challenges the deadness of the world – is primarily linked to the artist as desecrator.[13] Robert's desire to expose the guilty secrets of those around him eventually results in his aspiring to write a novel. Rather like Lister and her other villainous manipulators, Robert is the novelist's dark double who 'plan[s] the reactions' (*TR* 201) of those he encounters. His macabre orchestration of the book culminates in the 'beautiful harshness' (*TR* 222) of Lina's dance which, in theory, counters a rampant materialism. But, in stark contrast to the Abbess of Crewe, his ruthless opportunism makes it difficult for the reader not to see him as totally mired in a wholly benighted world.

For all their concern with the malaise of the present, Spark's fiction in the 1970s was also peculiarly concerned with the effects of the past. These effects may take the form of ghosts which refuse to be exorcised, as in *The Hothouse by the East River*, or the idea of whole epochs determined by the Holy Spirit, as in *The Abbess of Crewe*, or by the state of nature, as in *The Takeover*. After *Territorial Rights*, Spark no longer promotes an idea of redemption – whether it be religious or artistic – which can contain her abiding sense of disorder. For this reason, she goes back to a sense of madness, singularity and unrestrained emotion which prevailed before she endeavoured to turn her life into an untroubled and impersonal narrative. From now on, she is able to fully embrace the originary histories of her unconverted self.

7

Hauntings: The Return of the Repressed

Muriel Spark's previous four novels all include a version of history which helps to disrupt the certainties of the present day. These books alternate between a construction of the past which is literal – as in the traumatic histories of the Second World War in *The Hothouse by the East River* and *Territorial Rights* – or other-worldly – as in the idea of the era of the Holy Spirit in *The Abbess of Crewe* or the new paganism in *The Takeover*. But whether her view of these originary histories is naturalized or idealized, what is clear is that her fiction is increasingly haunted by the ghosts of the past. Her next three books, *Loitering with Intent* (1981), *The Only Problem* (1984) and *A Far Cry from Kensington* (1988), all return Spark to the 1940s and 1950s and to a more intimate sense of her origins. The immediate post-war period, as we have already seen, is part of Spark's prehistory which culminated in her double conversion in 1954 to Roman Catholicism and to the novel form. In more focused and biographical terms than ever before, her novels of the 1980s explore her formation as a writer and the unruly forces which needed to be banished to enable her to create fiction.

Spark's work in the 1970s can be said to have portrayed society, from a disdainful distance, as essentially irredeemable. By this time, she had simply given up on a redemptive narrative which could bring order to the chaos of the contemporary world. In her fiction published in the 1980s, however, her awareness of an abiding sense of disorder is less an external social question than an issue concerning the inner workings of the self. This can be seen principally in relation to the conversionist orthodoxy which was meant to have resolved the confusion inherent in her hybrid identity – part English, part Scottish, part Protestant, part Jewish. Rather than attempt to transcend such contradictions, as she did at the beginning of her career, Spark has begun gradually to relish an untransfigured self. This can be seen, for instance, in *Territorial Rights* where conversion is, implicitly, no longer an adequate response to a character's Jewishness. In this work, the anti-Semitic Lina Pancev unwittingly sleeps with a Jewish man and, once she learns of this, jumps into a nearby Venetian canal so as to rid herself of any potential racial contamination. But, instead of purifying her, the canal waters turn out to contain a high risk of infection and Lina has to take to her bed with antibiotics. By the 1980s, no amount of baptism can expunge the infectious and impure presence of the unconverted self from either life or art.

One of the most important of the later works, *Loitering with Intent* explores the narrative of renewal which had hitherto contained Spark's life-story. In her influential discussion with Frank Kermode, Spark made explicit the connection between her 'wasted' (*HF* 132) early life and her redemptive artistry. In these terms, as we have already seen, the first half of her life is reduced to a scene of muddle and disorder which needs to be transmuted into narrative. *Loitering with Intent* precisely challenges this restorative model of a life transfigured which distinguishes, above all, between the self before and after conversion. As Spark herself was to become aware, the abiding problem with this oversimple model of conversion is that it unproblematically ruptures the self into old and new or inner and outer. For an author who is on the side of unification or desegregation, a life-story which is centred around a split self is clearly untenable.

Loitering with Intent is not an autobiographical novel, as is often thought, but is a fictional rewriting of Spark's personal history so as to bring together both her converted and unconverted selves. It is one of her most playful and reflective works because it returns the reader not only to the content of *The Comforters* but also to its experimental form which self-consciously probes the nature of fiction-making. As John Updike and others have noted, there are elaborate similarities between Spark's first and sixteenth books which include the floral names of Caroline Rose and Fleur Talbot, the Queen's Gate location and the fact that both personae are neurotically writing their début novels on the 'grubby edge' (*LWI* 78) of literary London. There are also clear correspondences between many of the minor characters in these works such as Louisa Jebb and Lady Edwina Oliver or Georgina Hogg and Dottie Carpenter. But Updike is probably overstating his case when he argues that these two books occupy the 'same grid of concerns' or 'area of experience'.[1] To be sure, *Loitering with Intent* is written in the first person, a style not used since *Robinson*, and returns the reader to her own detailed life-history, which has not been evoked since *The Hothouse by the East River*. But, unlike these earlier works, *Loitering with Intent* is a meta-narrative which does not merely incorporate aspects of Spark's biography but radically interrogates the assumptions that lie behind the retelling of her life-story.

The novel begins with Spark's heroine – rightly characterized by Updike as more 'alter' than 'ego' – loitering ghost-like in a graveyard writing a poem. As is stressed from the start, this is the 'middle of the twentieth century' (to be precise 30 June 1950), a time which constitutes, for Fleur, 'the last day of a whole chunk of my life' (*LWI* 7). The division between the two halves of the century, as well as the living and the dead, significantly also coincides with the 'changing-point in [Fleur's] life' (*LWI* 143) when she moves from being a nascent to an accomplished artist. To enact her fissured self, both the subject and object of the novel, the wasted years of the younger Fleur are narrated by the redeemed older Fleur. This story is, in turn, refracted through the younger Fleur's work-in-progress, *Warrender Chase*, as well as her author's already known life-history and aesthetic philosophy. The younger Fleur becomes secretary to Sir Quentin Oliver, who runs the Autobiographical Association (a familiar cultish grouping) which relates to Spark's activities, between 1947 and 1949, with the Poetry Society and a publicity agent. But, if this novel supposedly conforms to Spark's life-history, it is also knowingly fictive and spends a good deal of time, with lavish reference to John Henry Newman and Benvenuto Cellini, exploring different and competing ways of writing life-histories.

On the one hand, *Loitering with Intent* playfully sets up a series of displacements so that the distinction between fact, fiction and fantasy is made deliberately unstable. In a typical reversal of the tenets of realist fiction (which is supposed to reflect reality), the younger Fleur, not unlike Caroline Rose, finds herself caught between madness and prophecy as her novel-within-a-novel appears to be conjuring up actual events.[2] In fact, by the end of the book, it becomes apparent that the plot of *Warrender Chase* has mysteriously prefigured much of Fleur's genuine experiences. The criminal machinations of Sir Quentin (which include drugging and blackmailing), and his demise in a car crash, eventually correspond to the story-line of her imagined *bête noire*, Warrender Chase. As with Dougal Douglas before her, Fleur fictionalizes the memoirs of those in the Autobiographical Association to make them more lifelike, but finally regards their actual lives as mere fabrications. Troubled by her 'very pious, old-fashioned Catholic' (*LWI* 91) friend and sparring partner, Dottie, she constantly questions her sanity and moral integrity as she considers those around her to be 'inventions of my own' (*LWI* 26). For this reason the younger Fleur, especially when found loitering in a graveyard, lays herself open to the accusation that the novelist's arts are a form of demonology, as she seems to be able to call up apparitions and give them a 'spurious materiality'.[3]

From Georgina Hogg onwards, Spark has included a particular kind of 'same as' Catholic with which to contrast her 'different-from' heroines. In the case of the appropriately named Dottie (here orthodoxy is essentially a form of neurosis) Fleur maintains that 'if her faith was true then mine was false' (*LWI* 47). What is more, although Fleur, unlike Caroline, is not a recent convert to Catholicism, Dottie spends a good deal of time attempting to reclaim Fleur as one of the righteous by using the language of conversionist orthodoxy. She secretly enrols her young friend in the 'Guild of Our Lady of Ransom' whose notepaper is headed 'for the Conversion of England. Jesus Convert England' which Fleur dismisses as 'claptrap' (*LWI* 92). Encouraged by Sir Quentin, Dottie accuses Fleur of being a 'fiend' (*LWI* 123) or 'witch' who has been 'sent to bring ideas into...life' (*LWI* 140) and who has 'plotted and planned' (*LWI* 156) the demise of those around her. Dottie advises Fleur to see a priest which Fleur pointedly dismisses: 'there are very few predicaments in a writer's life where it would be the slightest use explaining the ins and outs to a priest' (*LWI* 123). Most cutting of all to the younger Fleur, because it is an unstated fear,

Dottie describes her as an unwomanly intellectual whose 'head rules your heart' (*LWI* 21) and who keeps 'wriggling out of real life' (*LWI* 158). Much of the novel is spent by Fleur attempting to answer Dottie's false accusations.

Not unlike Caroline, the younger Fleur finds herself in a state of absolute confusion as she attempts to find a middle ground between Dottie's doctrinaire certainties and the free flow of her own 'instinctive' (*LWI* 19) creativity which, when unchecked, borders on delirium: 'I was tuning into voices without really hearing them as one does when moving from programme to programme on a wireless set' (*LWI* 81). Fleur desperately needs to distinguish herself from Sir Quentin, whom she thinks of as a figure of 'pure evil' (*LWI* 120), as her secretive and manipulative relationship to the members of the Autobiographical Association reflects his. In fact, at one point in the novel they are brought together in the same terms as she denounces Sir Quentin for 'stealing my myth. Without a mythology, a novel is nothing'. She goes on to declare, crucially, that 'the true novelist, one who understands the work as a continuous poem, is a myth-maker ... and the methods are mythological by nature' (*LWI* 100). Both Sir Quentin and Fleur are not dissimilar myth-makers who, as the novel's title makes clear, engage in the criminal activity of 'loitering with intent'. The demonic potential of art, realized most completely by Sir Quentin, is made clear from the beginning when Fleur, just after she leaves the graveyard, describes the '*demon* inside me that rejoiced in seeing people as they were' (*LWI* 8).

Apart from the autobiographical investment in the book, Fleur is shown on one level to be no different from Spark's other mythomaniacs – such as Jean Brodie, Lister, or the Abbess of Crewe – who, as novelists manqués, attempt to shape reality according to their abiding myths. In relation to Sir Quentin, Fleur has been rightly said to 'summon up apparitions to fight apparitions', which results in the writer's creative process being akin to a 'demonological battle with her subject'.[4] Sir Quentin, after all, insists on 'absolute frankness' (*LWI* 74) from his quasi-religious grouping which, like Fleur, he then shapes into a purely instrumental or blackmailing narrative. To distinguish herself absolutely from both Dottie's dogmatism and Sir Quentin's rapacious need for disclosure, the older Fleur applies the language of morality and redemption to her own fiction-making so as to contain the disparate voices in her head. Echoing the Kermode interview, almost verbatim in parts, she claims that 'everything happens to an artist; time is always redeemed, nothing is lost and wonders will never cease' (*LWI* 83). At other times, Fleur talks about picking out key phrases from 'the wreckage of the moment' (*LWI* 36) so that her art not only transfigures the commonplace but also the writer herself. This is clear from the momentous declaration in the novel when the younger and older Fleur, both subject and object, are united in the following terms:

> But in the departure of the Autobiographical Association I felt I had escaped from [the past]. Although in reality I wasn't yet rid of Sir Quentin and his little sect, they were morally outside of myself, they were objectified. I would write about them one day. In fact, under one form or another, whether I have liked it or not, I have written about them ever since, the straws from which I have made my bricks. (*LWI* 141–2)

As with a redemptive narrative, which too neatly resolves all of the younger Fleur's uncertainties, this assertion of god-like impersonality, which objectifies and moralizes the world, is refuted in much of the novel. The quest for impersonality, on the one hand, results in Sir Quentin's 'little sect' becoming the originary scene for the younger Fleur which she, from then on, transforms into the universal language of art ('the straws from which I have made my bricks'). But there is something rather inhuman in this proclamation of objectivity which turns fiction-making, in Fleur's 'light and heartless hand' (*LWI* 59), into a kind of monstrous revenge. For this reason, one critic has taken Spark at her word and claimed implausibly that Fleur is, not unlike the dead body in *Territorial Rights*, literally a ghost from the graveyard haunting the novel.[5] As Fleur considers 'human character' (*LWI* 30) to be essentially contradictory and para-doxical, the too easy transcendence of her fissured self – as either artist or ghost – is clearly at the cost of her own conflicted humanity. What is more, given Fleur's definition of art as essentially ambiguous and amoral (*LWI* 53) – much to Dottie's horror – there is a sense in which her own search for moral certainty will, in the most profound sense, make her work lifeless.

Spark clearly understands the brutality inherent in the narrative unification of the younger and older Fleur and so she fills her novel with a demonic counter-narrative which stresses those unconverted elements of the 'human character' which cannot be contained or transfigured. This counter-narrative can be seen especially in the figures of Edwina Oliver and Solly Mendelsohn who embody those unruly forces which Spark at first wished to expunge. Sir Quentin's mother Edwina, with her 'red talons' (*LWI* 18) and shrewd advice is, notably, a 'splendid apparition...an ancient, wrinkled, painted spirit wrapped in luxurious furs' (*LWI* 38). Along with Edwina, Fleur relies on the foul-mouthed but lovable poet, Solly Mendelsohn – with his 'huge bulk', 'great Semitic head' (*LWI* 55), and 'night-pale face' (*LWI* 157) – to define an incongruous humanity beyond the constraints laid down by Dottie and Sir Quentin. Echoing many of Spark's own pronouncements, Fleur defines her different-from Catholicism with the following: 'I simply didn't have the time or the mentality for guilds and indulgences, fasts and feasts and observances' (*LWI* 92). She gains a macabre sense of spirituality from Edwina and Solly which, as in the paganism of *The Takeover*, is on the side of anarchic incongruity. Following on from Spark's most recent female figures such as Maggie Radcliffe, Annabel Christopher or Cathy Klopstock, Fleur's stress on her instinctive or spontaneous artistry combines a pre-social state of nature with a necessary artistic detachment.

Edwina and Solly are, above all else, benign pagan spirits who are on the side of unconfined 'inexplicable life' (*LWI* 42) and are the very opposite of the order and stability brought about by a transfiguring conversionism. They are both demonic figures who bring together Spark's part-Jewishness and the 'demon' inside Fleur which 'rejoiced' in 'seeing people as they were' (*LWI* 8). In the end, the writer's arts are associated with poetic spontaneity, individual instinct and 'chance grace' (*LWI* 158), rather than a coldly impersonal transcendence of a 'wasted' world. As if to stress the limits inherent in her quest for an 'external' (*LWI* 129) vision, Fleur, after rejecting such a vision, immediately registers her sense of joy and wonder at being 'a woman and artist in the twentieth century' (*LWI* 129). With this thought Spark's heroine, at regular intervals, goes 'on my way rejoicing', a refrain which is also used at the end of Spark's autobiography (*CV* 213) and helps to set the optimistic tone of the novel.

With remarkable economy, Spark does not merely frame the difficulties in constructing a narrative in relation to her own refracted early life but extends it to the question of autobiography in general. She does this by citing at length the lives of both Benvenuto Cellini and John Henry Newman as possible models for those in the Autobiographical Association. As Newman's *Apologia pro vita sua* was a key influence in persuading Spark to convert to Catholicism in 1954, his place in this book is clearly significant. Fleur's rejection of Newman – on the grounds that his 'I-and-thou relationship to God' meant that he was to 'doubt the reality of the rest of life' (*LWI* 70) – is particularly telling in this regard. Spiritual conversion alone, in this rereading, ignores the 'rest of life' which cannot be so easily expunged. In contrast, Benvenuto Cellini's *Life*, which initially used the phrase 'on my way rejoicing' (*LWI* 90), is 'robust and full-blooded' (*LWI* 75) and is fully conscious of the artistry necessary in the making of a life-story. While Newman unites his youthful and matured selves through his 'neurotic' (*LWI* 70) relationship with God, Cellini is 'comically contradictory' (*LWI* 89), recognizing a range of possible selves. Fleur, in the end, rejects the 'awful madness' (*LWI* 69) inherent in Newman's homogenizing narrative.

As Laura Marcus has rightly argued, autobiographical discourses can be open and transgressive – challenging the distinctions between fact and fiction or subject and object – but they can, equally, be a 'magical instrument of reconciliation'.[6] Spark's *Loitering with Intent* includes simultaneously both possibilities although, as her rejection of Newman makes plain, she no longer needs to reconcile the different versions of herself into a single unified story. Those, such as Sir Quentin and Dottie, who believe in only one fixed explanation of the world are ultimately figures of evil who deny the artistic spirit. The dilemma for Spark is that as a Catholic, and self-confessed mythologizer, she might well be implicated in their moral depravity. In her next book, *The Only Problem*, Spark looks at the question of evil in relation to the book of Job and thinks of figures such as Sir Quentin and Dottie primarily as comforters or misleading reality instructors. While *The Only Problem* does not draw openly on Spark's experiences during the 1950s, it expressly refers back to her close interest in the book of Job. In 1953, Spark was said to be writing an extended study of Job which resulted in her 1955 essay, 'The Mystery of Job's Suffering', as well as the title of her first novel, *The Comforters*.

Loitering with Intent constructed a public version of Spark's experience in the late 1940s and early 1950s which was primarily concerned with her formation as a novelist. By comparison, *The Only Problem* evokes her inner turmoil at this point and, in particular, the question of theodicy or whether one can have faith in a divine providence that is the 'actual author' (*OP* 19) of suffering in the world. It is this problem – 'the only problem, in fact, worth discussing' (*OP* 19) – which obsesses Spark's Job-like protagonist, Harvey Gotham. A Canadian millionaire in his mid-30s, Harvey is writing a study of the book of Job and, after abandoning his wife Effie in Italy, settles in a cottage in the South of France to complete his work. On one level, he could not be further from the conventional Sparkian heroine such as Caroline Rose or Fleur Talbot. Wealthy and male, his surname associates him with the traditional foolish town of Gotham and there are elements of his study, such as his research into the eyelids of crocodiles, which are absurdly literal. At the same time, many of his conclusions regarding the book of Job – that it is 'shockingly amoral' (*OP* 67), 'the pivotal book of the Bible' (OP 67), and an unknowable 'poem' (*OP* 132) – echo Spark's own essay, even, at one point, word for word: '[Job] not only argued the problem of suffering, he suffered the problem of argument' (*OP* 30).

In less obvious ways than *Loitering with Intent*, *The Only Problem* continues to deal with fundamental questions concerning the relationship between Spark's unconverted suffering self and her supposedly redeemed later self. The version of Job in this novel is, in fact, not unlike Spark's own breakdown in the 1950s (which is reflected in the babble of 'voices' which Caroline and the younger Fleur hear). Harvey believes, at various times in the novel, that Job was 'having a nervous crisis' (*OP* 32) and was 'like a patient on the couch' (*OP* 53); or, that Job 'had a sort of nervous breakdown' (*OP* 68) which 'reduced' him to a 'mental and physical wreck' (*OP* 78). When thinking of Job's three comforters, he imagines them taking 'turns as analyst' (*OP* 53), which may be an implicit reference to Spark's own curative

Jungian therapy in the 1950s. To this extent, Harvey's self-conscious parallels with the figure of Job – his temporary penury, the manifold sufferings caused by Effie's terrorist activities, his interfering 'comforters' (*OP* 49) – place him in the same Job-like position as Caroline or Fleur. All are trying to order their fragmented lives through their writing while being subject to the chaos of other unknown and unwelcome stories. In Harvey's case, his theories concerning the book of Job are distorted by the world's media, and his scholarly seclusion in the South of France is turned into a paranoid fantasy by his police interrogators.

From the beginning, Spark did not want to turn the book of Job into a specifically Christian allegory which Carl Gustav Jung's *Answer to Job* (1952), in particular, was at pains to argue. Her essay on 'The Mystery of Job's Suffering' was, for the most part, an extended review of *Answer to Job* which was, in turn, Jung's implicit answer to the charge of anti-Semitism and Nazi collaboration levelled against him.[7] In her essay, Spark rejected as being 'far too anthropomorphic to be satisfying' Jung's belief that God's 'collision with Job' (MJS 7) is fulfilled in the incarnation. This argument is repeated in *The Only Problem* when Harvey's 'puritanical' (*OP* 179) Aunt Pet contends that there is a 'Christian message in the *Book of Job*' (*OP* 136). Harvey objects to this statement with the following retort, 'but Job didn't know that' (*OP* 136). In other words, Harvey, like Spark before him, does not want to impose a redemptive narrative on the formless and unstructured book of Job which has been rightly described as a 'demonic parody' of Genesis. Harold Fisch is close to the spirit of Spark's novel when he maintains that the book of Job is haunted by 'the image of a monstrous world . . . a world of eerie shapes and nightmares, of unimaginable gulfs, and of great creatures of the deep [which] refuse to submit themselves to man'.[8] In these terms, the book of Job is resistant to exegesis of all kinds and only Job's comforters mistakenly try and make sense of the universe by mythologizing it.

One crucial context for Spark's particular investment in the nightmarish book of Job in the early 1950s, at the time of her conversion, is what Harvey calls the 'unspeakable sufferings of the world' (*OP* 19). The stark disjunction between Spark's embrace of the Catholic faith, shortly after the bloodshed and misery caused by the Second World War, is a fraught aspect of a number of her books. *The Girls of Slender Means*, on the one hand, rejects all forms of secular renewal, whereas *The Mandelbaum Gate* evokes the unimaginable dimensions of the Holocaust to indicate the severe limitations on the spiritual transfiguration of human suffering. As she shows in her story 'The First Year of My Life' (1967), the fact that Spark was born in 1918, at the height of the carnage of the First World War, makes the problem of death and rebirth an especially intimate question. Part of Harvey's foolishness is to express a theory which can somehow embrace misery on this vast historical scale which, in the end, is absurdly deterministic: 'the individual soul has made a pact with God before he is born, that he will suffer during his lifetime.... Sufferers would, in this hypothesis, be pre-conscious volunteers. The same might apply to tribes or nations, especially in the past' (*OP* 27). The shift from the 'individual' to the 'tribe or nation' is particularly troubling as it confuses personal anguish with a much broader collective history.

While Harvey recognizes that his 'distress' (*OP* 180) does not make him a 'prophet' (*OP* 124), he does play with the idea that he is a Job-figure, which enables him to take account of suffering not only of himself but of the world as a whole. As with many of Spark's personae, beginning with Caroline Rose and January Marlow, Harvey wants to get 'outside' (*OP* 179) of his own experiences to connect up with those beyond his (largely privileged) individual sphere. To this extent he is described in idealized Sparkian terms as being both 'detached and involved at the same time' (*OP* 28) and vehemently protests against those who 'conspire...to estrange [him] from suffering' (*OP* 64). In a key scene in the book, he notices a 'lean-faced man with a dark skin' (*OP* 152) who appears to be a refugee from the Balkans. This figure throws into relief his own dangerously self-centred sense of discomfort:

> It was not the first time Harvey had noticed that poor people from Eastern Europe resembled...the poor of Western Europe years ago.... Patience, pallor and deep anxiety: there goes suffering, Harvey reflected. And I found him interesting. Is it only by recognising how flat would be the world without the sufferings of others that we know how desperately becalmed our own lives would be without suffering?.... But *Job*, my work on *Job*, all interrupted

and neglected, probed into and interfered with: that is experience, too... To study, to think, is to live and suffer painfully. (*OP* 153)

Harvey, significantly, once again foolishly conflates his own experiences with a more widespread suffering. He curiously leaves open the ways in which a writer's life – rather 'flat' or 'desperately becalmed' without a certain amount of distress – can be equated with the calamities of the world as a whole. One should not underestimate, with regard to his solipsism, the connection made between the poor of Eastern and Western Europe. The journey from east to west, after all, recalls not only the pre-war migrations of European Jewry (including Spark's paternal grandparents) but also the struggle of post-war Soviet Jewry to emigrate out of Stalinist Russia (in which Spark took an active interest). Even the description of the refugee as 'dark skinned' relates to the Italian-Jewish Leo in *Territorial Rights* with his 'Afro-frizzed hair' (*TR* 92) as well as Spark's 'white negress' (*CS* 309) grandmother in 'The Gentile Jewesses'. The historical resonances evoked by this East European figure throw into pointed relief Harvey's insistence on relating such vast misery to his own plight as an author.

Some of Spark's readers, such as Gabriel Josipovici, have concurred fully with Harvey, noting that, in these terms, writing is 'suffering and joy combined, for it entails the daily struggle to shed cliché and habit'.[9] What is interesting about this reading is that it is a much more accurate description of the younger Fleur who attempts exhaustively to shed the malign (because predictable) influences on her fiction of those around her. Where Harvey differs from Fleur is precisely in attempting to go beyond the solipsism of the artist. Because of Harvey's over-weening preoccupation with 'the only problem', Spark seems to be concerned less with the struggles of writing, and the search for a unique vision, than with the difficulties of moving imaginatively beyond the self. Fleur's struggle to objectify her experiences is an artistic version of Harvey's quest to situate himself in the wider world of pain. While Fleur recognizes the value of her own formative suffering in shaping her into a successful novelist, Harvey's presumed empathy with historical misery is, in the end, something of a romantic fallacy. Spark exposes his affectation most forcefully with reference to the ghostly presence of his wife Effie who, although estranged from him, is in Harvey's thoughts almost as much as the figure of Job.

Effie is an extreme example of a mythomaniac who wishes to turn her particular obsessions into an account of the world as a whole. Her insistence on linking petty theft to the search for global justice is symptomatic of this inflated desire which Harvey, at first, rejects completely. To this extent, she mitigates his own facile shift from the self to the world and also helps him understand that he is not, unlike Hubert Mallindaine, promoting a 'new religion' (*OP* 136). As both Josipovici and Frank Kermode have shown at some length, what is notable about Harvey's version of the book of Job is the role played, compared to the original, by Job's wife who is closely identified with Effie.[10] The reason Harvey moves to the village of St Dié is that it is near to Epinal, which he visits frequently to see Georges de la Tour's 'sublime painting, *Job Visited by his Wife*' (*OP* 75). His view of Effie's terrorist activities is refracted through this painting to the extent that, after her death, he believes that she looks exactly like de la Tour's wife of Job. Her death is objectified through this picture and helps Harvey to end his rather neurotic obsession with 'the only problem'.

Like Maggie Radcliffe, Effie at first 'boils down to money' (*OP* 41), and her violent pursuit of 'justice' is deemed by Harvey to be essentially materialistic, 'there is more to be had from the world than a balancing of accounts' (*OP* 42). Her terroristic behaviour is the dark side of her 'anarchistic, aristocratic' (*OP* 61) nature which Harvey remains in love with. She is, in other words, described as if she were a demonic Abbess of Crewe who is simultaneously both life-enhancing and death-inducing. Harvey's love for her, unlike his romantic quasi-suffering, has a supposed 'objective quality' (*OP* 18) which, not unlike the Sparkian novelist, enables him to move from grand theories of the universe to a more profound exploration of the ambiguities of a single individual. In a repetition of the ending of *The Public Image*, Harvey adopts Effie's infant, and has a new baby with her sister Ruth, which returns him to the by now familiar pre-social state of nature. Echoing the epilogue to the book of Job, Harvey aims to 'live another hundred and forty years [with his] three daughters, Clara, Jemima and Eye-Paint' (*OP* 189). The ghostly Effie, a distinctly paradoxical version of feminine grace, helps to transform Harvey so that he is once again on the side of life.

What is significant about the spiritual and aesthetic reclamation of Effie is that it does not result in a straightforward 'happy ending' (*OP* 186). In fact, Harvey describes Job's epilogue as a 'tragedy' (*OP* 186) as it finally removes suffering from the biblical story. As Josipovici rightly notes, the possibility that Effie is living in a Californian commune, having avoided being killed in Paris, does effectively illustrate the flattening consequences of a story without pain. In *Memento Mori* (1959), Henry Mortimer also recognized that 'Without an ever-present sense of death life is insipid. You might as well live on the whites of eggs' (*MM* 150). Spark, in this way, struggles with the redemptive necessity of death and anguish – so that her writing is not bland – as well as with the irredeemable horrors of the First and Second World Wars. In these terms, there is an unresolved tension between Harvey's final Job-like and mysterious state of grace – 'beyond the reach of discourse' (MJS 7) – and the overwhelming proximity of a tormented world. Spark's next novel, *A Far Cry from Kensington*, although far less achieved than her previous two books, continues the exploration of an originary suffering in relation to her formation as an artist. Once again, a personal history of discomfort and distress clashes awkwardly with an impersonal narrative of renewal.

One way of reading *A Far Cry from Kensington* is as an uneasy amalgam of her last two novels. On the one hand, as most of its reviewers have noted, it closely follows *Loitering with Intent* with regard to its autobiographical subtext in mid-1950s South Kensington. The book's Catholic heroine, Mrs Nancy Hawkins, is on the fringes of literary London and has many affinities with her author, such as her time spent in southern Africa and a brief marriage that has come to grief.[11] At the same time, the book directly follows *The Only Problem* as it contains a good deal of post-war trauma which includes the suicide of a Polish refugee, Wanda Polodok, and references to such figures as Cathy, a 'concentration camp' (*FC* 15) survivor, who regularly threatens to put her 'head in the gas oven' (*FC* 54). The 'upsurge of interest in the supernatural', a key element in the novel, is also ascribed to the 'uncontemplatable events which had blackened the previous decade' (*FC* 104). Although Nancy Hawkins's quaint lodging house does recall *The Girls of Slender Means*, Spark is at pains to situate a disturbing European or cosmopolitan perspective at the heart of an ostensibly conventional English setting.

Like Harvey, Nancy spends much of the book contemplating her connection with the recent histories of mass murder and enforced exile, especially as embodied by Wanda whose 'capacity for suffering verged on rapacity' (FC 7). The corpulent but sympathetic 'Mrs Hawkins', who opens the novel, eventually 'decided to be thin' (FC 10) on the selfish grounds that she would no longer feel 'spooky, empty, haunted' (FC 130) by the emotional demands of those around her. Much of the book concerns the transformation of the overweight 'Mrs Hawkins' into the light-weight 'Nancy' whose new-found slenderness indicates that she has rather mercilessly discarded the troubles of her many previous confidantes. Once again, Spark sets up a split self (with the thin Nancy recollecting her fat counterpart) and has most of the action taking place between 1954 and 1955, the year of her own transfiguration. Along with the redoubled Nancy Hawkins, Spark introduces an idealized version of herself in the guise of the majestically successful novelist, Emma Loy. One reviewer noted that 'these two women may seem to make one Muriel Spark', except that what these various figures do is irredeemably fragment Spark.[12] Unlike *Loitering with Intent*, this book does not propose a unified narrative but crystallizes in one text entirely different renderings of the author.

Although Nancy attempts to shed the weight of the past, she opens the novel at night unable to sleep and is surrounded by 'darkness, thought, memory, sweet anticipations' (FC 5). Her semi-conscious 'night-watch' (FC 6) means that her thoughts move, in acknowledged Proustian fashion, from day into night, or from order into chaos, and it is this movement which eventually becomes a kind of anti-conversion. At the beginning of the book, Mrs Hawkins regularly recites the 'Angelus at twelve noon' (FC 51) but, by the end, she regards her 'compulsive Hail Marys at twelve o'clock noon' as a form of 'mad . . . superstition' (FC 127). What is more, she replaces her orthodox rituals with the heterodox but equally ritualistic denouncement of the 'hack writer', Hector Bartlett, as a *'pisseur de copie'* or 'urinator of journalistic copy' (FC 45). Hector turns out to be the familiar Sparkian cultist and blackmailer whose bizarre activities, not unlike those of Sir Quentin before him, result in the suicide of one of his members, the rapaciously agonized Wanda. Whereas Caroline Rose pointedly overcomes her not dissimilar 'rapacity for suffering' (*C* 38), Wanda is unable to withstand Hector's onslaught. After Wanda's death, Hector is the one figure who unites Nancy and Emma Loy. While he is primarily a buffoon, and thus somewhat over-determined as a figure of evil, it is clear from a reading of Spark's autobiography (*CV* 186–92) that Hector had the same parasitic relationship with Emma as Derek Stanford had with Spark herself.

Nancy's insistence on exposing Hector at every opportunity as a '*pisseur de copie*' is said to feel 'like preaching the gospel' (*FC* 110). Her new credo ultimately results in Nancy vengefully 'settl[ing] the bill' (*FC* 189) with her somewhat ludicrous *bête noire*. This decidedly secular form of poetic justice is, in Harvey Gotham's terms, no more than a materialistic 'balancing of accounts' (*OP* 42). It is, above all, a markedly aberrant form of ritual, not unlike those of Spark's more palpable mythomaniacs, except that it is on the side of artistic worth. Like Fleur, Nancy is engaged in a demonological battle with evil which means that, apart from her all-important shrewdness and intelligence, there is very little difference between her new religion and those of more obviously depraved figures. Because the slim-line Nancy is so troubling a heroine, not unlike the equally unpleasant Sandy Stranger, Emma Loy becomes necessary as a less ambiguous (if slightly smug) representative of artistic grace. The solipsism and brutality of Nancy Hawkins, in the end, have to be displaced onto the 'magic and...charm' (*FC* 98) of Emma Loy.

At this late point in her career, Spark is able to look at her own practices as a novelist with a painful honesty. One is struck, especially, by the astonishing number of references to her early work, such as 'You Should Have Seen the Mess' (1958) or 'The Black Madonna' (1958) or her African stories, and to her many subsequent novels. There are also detailed allusions to some of the key authors who have influenced her, such as Mary Shelley and Proust. It is as if Spark has to construct a textual homeland in order to act as a barrier against the ghostly forces from the past which constantly haunt her and remind her of a time of uncontrolled suffering. This is not exactly a form of artistic salvation but she does seem to find some comfort in settling old scores with the injustices of the past. As her next two books will show, she is able to embrace both her converted and unconverted selves, which seems to be the best way that she knows of remedying the nightmare of history.

8

Continuities and Discontinuities

Muriel Spark's next two novels, *Symposium* (1990) and *Reality and Dreams* (1996), return the reader to the more impersonal and minimalist mode which was first encountered in *Memento Mori* (1959) and which reached its apotheosis in much of her best work such as *The Public Image* (1968), *The Driver's Seat* (1970), *Not to Disturb* (1971) and *The Abbess of Crewe* (1974). Throughout her writing career, Spark has always challenged the assumptions and preoccupations of her previous books. She is continually in dialogue with herself and it is unsurprising, after her many imaginative meditations on her early life in post-war London, that her most recent fiction has once again eschewed her life-story. With the publication of her first volume of autobiography in 1992, dealing with similar material to *Loitering with Intent* (1981) and *A Far Cry from Kensington* (1988), there is a clear exhaustion with the artistic reclamation of her wasted or unconverted life. The pattern of Spark's career, beginning with her first two books, is to veer in and out of her biography and to move from a distinct persona to an impersonal narrative voice. Just as she questions the nature of autobiographical recollections in her fiction of the 1980s, she plays with the supposed power and command of authorial omniscience in her current works.

Most of Spark's critics have mistakenly thought of her as an unchanging moralist who has been absorbed by the same eternal verities since her conversion. A good many studies of Spark's fiction have concluded, with remarkable similarity, that she is 'writing in the great moral tradition of British literature' or that her novels are written '*sub specie aeternitatis*' (under the light of eternity) and are 'primarily concerned with the relationship between God and man'. Alan Bold is the notable exception to this rule as he has rightly qualified the presumed continuities within her supposed moral vision by noting her fundamental misgivings towards both her faith and the novel form.[1] *Symposium* and *Reality and Dreams* confirm this sceptical reading, with the protagonist of the latter novel claiming that he no longer believes in 'convictions' as they are 'generally hypocrisy' (*RD* 29). Nonetheless, for all their perversity, both of these late works knowingly utilize a familiar story-line concerning a delightfully small world which is then disrupted by an uncanny stranger who is also a purveyor of fictions. With few exceptions – such as the more expansive *The Mandelbaum Gate* (1965), *The Takeover* (1976) and *Territorial Rights* (1979) – Spark has relied on stunning variations of this literary model throughout her career. By the 1990s she was well aware of her novelistic foibles in this regard and, thus, sets up a customary pattern of expectations only to rudely dash them.

Symposium especially recalls *The Ballad of Peckham Rye* (1960) in its evocation of the border ballad tradition of Scottish writing with its emotionally charged supernatural resonances. Educated at Edinburgh University, Dougal Douglas is, as Bold has noted, a 'peculiarly Scottish devil' who dances the Highland fling, claims to have Highland blood, and has many diabolical features taken from folk conventions.[2] He exposes the emptiness of those he encounters and, though obviously a mythological figure, appears ironically to be more rounded than his ostensibly realistic counterparts. In a similar vein, Spark throughout *Territorial Rights* gave special prominence to Anthea Leaver who dreams of her Ayrshire grandmother singing 'My Highland Lassie' (*TR* 51, 172, 237). This song, which enters Anthea's unconscious, offers up a series of heartfelt poetic insights – concerning love, longing and loss – and contrasts starkly with the unreal fabrications of most of the novel's dramatis personae. With reference to the apparently ghoulish figure of Margaret Damien (née Murchie), *Symposium* continues this use of the ballad tradition as an alternative means of perceiving the world. As with Dougal, the book revolves around the red-haired Margaret – perhaps a reference to the 'reddish hair' (*CV* 107) of Spark herself – whose family is from the Scottish borders. But, unlike Dougal, Margaret deliberately hides her demonic powers while appearing to be the only common-place character in the book.

Beginning with an epigraph from Lucian's *Symposium* – 'the party was finally broken up by the shedding of blood' (*S* 5) – Spark, in her nineteenth work, combines an extravagantly prepared dinner-party in Islington with the lethal machinations which surround it. She also cites as an epigraph the moment at the end of Plato's *Symposium* when Socrates insists that 'the true artist in tragedy was an artist in comedy also' (*S* 5). Spark, never easy to classify as a comic or serious writer, again shows that in this epigraph she is at pains to mix up absolutely everything in her fiction including her own basic assumptions. What is more, the Jewish Seder at the Passover feast, which Spark refers to extensively in *The Mandelbaum Gate* and 'The Gentile Jewesses' (1963), can be said to have been modelled on the symposia of Plato's Athens. Although she does not make these ancient connections explicit, the juxtaposition of Seder and Symposium is in the spirit of her characteristic quest to unite old and new, Jew and Greek.

The more mundane symposium or dinner-party which comprises the novel is made up of five cosmopolitan couples – hosts Hurley Reed and Chris Donovan, Ella and Ernst Untzinger, Lord and Lady Suzy, William and Margaret Damien, and cousins, Roland Sykes and Annabel Treece – who are tragically connected by the murder of Hilda Damien. In a typical series of flash-backs and flash-forwards, we begin to focus on the seemingly bland and sugary Margaret who, we soon learn, has 'inherited something wild' (*S* 81) from her insane Uncle Magnus. Mad Magnus, as he is known, is a key figure in the book as he is an 'imaginative factor' (*S* 65) and a 'guru and guide' (*S* 80), who recites border ballads to Margaret and connects her to a mythological history of transgression and difference: 'the Murchies of old were great cursers, oath-takers and foul-mouthers' (*S* 106). Not unlike Spark's insanely prophetic figures in *The Mandelbaum Gate*, Magnus claims to 'prognosticate and foreshadow. My divine affliction is your only guide' (*S* 81).

Margaret, according to Magnus, 'sees things double, treble, not as they really are' (*S* 106) and it is clear that she, like her uncle, has a skewed version of reality as well as 'the demonic will and single-minded purpose of the mad' (*S* 146). Not unlike Lise in *The Driver's Seat*, who also wears gaudily coloured clothes, Margaret aims to usurp the role of both her secular and her divine maker and attempts to wholly determine her fate. It turns out that she has been a 'passive carrier of disaster' (*S* 143) since her adolescence and that many of those close to her have met untimely ends. As a response to her so-called 'evil eye' (*S* 143), which she has no control over, she decides to 'actively make disasters come about' (*S* 144) and take her 'life and destiny in [her] own hands' (*S* 144). To this end, she plans to kill her mother-in-law, Hilda Damien, after tricking William, Hilda's exceedingly eligible son, into marriage. The clear implication of Margaret's new-found wilfulness is that it destroys the magical possibility, as with Fleur in *Loitering with Intent*, that her innate creativity might shape reality in remarkable and unexpected ways. By renouncing her true nature, so to speak, she becomes an inhuman demagogue who craves power over life and death. Magnus makes this clear when he responds to her bloodthirsty schemes by saying that 'the wish alone is evil' (*S* 144).

In his review of *Symposium*, Gabriel Josipovici fears that Spark is no longer treating the question of evil seriously as a 'kind of negation' – or form of 'self-love' and 'refusal of the imagination' – but is merely trivializing it as an external malediction.[3] Margaret's desire to determine her existence completely is, however, precisely a refusal of mystery or the artistic imagination. With poetic justice, her monomania is ultimately defeated when Spark introduces a secondary story-line which results in the death of Hilda Damien days before Margaret – who 'shrieks' (*S* 191) with frustration at the news – is able to 'liquidate' (*S* 159) her. This alternative narrative concerns a conspiracy of predatory servants, reminiscent of *Not to Disturb*, who use the dinner parties of the wealthy as a means of ascertaining when their houses will be empty and ripe for burglary. Hilda Damien, sharing a fate similar to that of Lettie Colston in *Memento Mori*, is murdered when she disturbs a thief in her house. Luke, a graduate student who waits at tables, masterminds this intrigue and, like Lauro in *The Takeover* exploits those he serves both sexually and financially. These conflicting plots, which converge on Hilda Damien, are both self-consciously bounded by Spark's previous work and turned into two essentially contrasting versions of evil which skilfully encompass and differentiate the writer.

The key distinction, with regard to these two clashing Sparkian plot-lines, is articulated at the end of *Territorial Rights* when Grace notes that the 'really professional evil-doers love it', as compared to the 'unhappy...guilty amateurs and the neurotics' (TR 235). Magnus says much the same thing when he speaks of truly 'guilty people' feeling 'exalted, triumphant, amused at themselves' (S 160). Luke's fun-loving criminals are, obviously, the triumphant professionals in this regard, and the guilt-ridden but potentially innocent Margaret, known finally as a 'female Jekyll and Hyde' (S 187), is the neurotic amateur. Before she attempts to take her fate in her own hands, the key mystery which surrounds Margaret's 'evil eye' is whether it is the actual author of the deaths which haunt her. Given that Spark has invested so much in associating the border tradition with her own poetic imagination, it is clear that Margaret, especially when she is brought together with Magnus, has a welcome demonic creativity. Margaret is not a writer manqué, because her powers remain external to her, but she does illustrate the dangerous necessity of invoking those super-natural and magical elements, reminiscent of Fleur Talbot, which are beyond any kind of control. When she attempts to become a 'professional evil-doer' she denies these forces at the cost of her own humanity.

As we have seen in *Loitering with Intent*, once Spark rejects a narrative of redemption, which too readily flattens out differ-ences of all kinds, she is prepared to take seriously the possibility that Fleur's amoral arts, not unlike Margaret's 'evil eye', are complicit with the depravity of the world. In *Symposium*, Spark's own history of otherness – such as an unruly Scottishness, and painful intimacy with insanity – is tacitly evoked by Margaret as *'La Philosophie des Autres'* (S 35), derived from the French-Jewish philosopher Emmanuel Levinas.[4] Mad Magnus, unlike Margaret who domesticates and prettifies the idea of *'Les Autres'*, becomes the perfect embodiment of Sparkian difference as his 'capacity for arranging his own life was formidable. It was only his overwhelming fits of wild and savage mania...that distinguished him from a normal Scottish eccentric' (S 144). The tension between an illusory life-arranging narrative and the mania beneath the surface can be said to characterize Spark's eccentric fiction in general and *Symposium* in particular. In a wonderful illustration of this mixture of anarchy and elegance, Spark includes an exaggerated version of the Abbey of Crewe, jokingly called the Convent of Good Hope, with three 'extremely individualistic' (*S* 109) nuns – foul-mouthed, mini-skirt wearing and Marxist – and the rest, 'dreary as hell' (*S* 103). While this may well be something of a self-parody, Spark clearly has a good deal of sympathy with these different-from nuns who hold in tension a transgressive otherness with a transcendent philosophy.

Although *Symposium* is on the side of disorder and heterodoxy – as shown by Mad Magnus's ironic belief that 'religious mania' is a kind of 'madness' (*S* 107) – *Reality and Dreams* attempts to make out a case for the importance of authorial control and omniscience. Spark is well aware of the brutality inherent in expunging that which cannot be assimilated into a consummate fiction. This was starkly illustrated in *Not to Disturb* where the all-seeing narrator clinically despatches characters who 'do not come into the story' (*ND* 31). There is a constant struggle in her work between the immediate demands of transforming life into an entertaining narrative and a messier sense of that which cannot so easily conform to the requirements of 'the story'. *Reality and Dreams* explicitly addresses this question by having as its central figure Tom Richards, a 63-year-old movie director who is constantly thinking about what and who should be included in his film. Spark pokes fun at his sense of god-like authority by having him fall off a tall crane while directing his latest creation. He is bed-bound for much of the novel and embodies its twin motifs of a feeling of redundancy, shared by virtually all of the characters in the book, and of having an all-consuming sense of unreality.

The opening of *Reality and Dreams* turns out to be a reprise of her previous two books as well as her work in general. Tom, for most of the first chapter, is unsure whether he is alive or dead and drifts in and out of consciousness trying to order the disparate voices that he hears from below. Both *A Far Cry from Kensington* and *Symposium* begin with Nancy Hawkins and Helen Suzy in an in-between state, uncertain of whether they are asleep or awake, with only a fragmentary sense of their existence. Their feelings of being haunted by reality, with characters in a ghost-like condition, is a familiar Sparkian trope which she has utilized since her earliest short stories. Tom repeatedly quotes the opening lines from T. S. Eliot's 'The Love Song of J. Alfred Prufrock' – '*Let us go then you and I*' (*RD* 75) or

'*Like a patient etherised upon a table*' (*RD* 78) – as if to stress both his sense of internal division and of being part of an 'insubstantial' (*RD* 64) dream. Patrick Parrinder's suggestion that Spark's art has anaesthetized the violence of reality seems especially pertinent in relation to Eliot's poetic image.[5] It is no coincidence, in this regard, that Eliot's first name is the same as Spark's sympathetic protagonist.

A key part of Tom's split identity is between his real and etherized self. On a conscious level, he is completely heartless, dismissing those around him as 'superfluous' (*RD* 13) or as a 'non-necessary person' (*RD* 27) and, in general, disposing of those whom he considers to be a 'thing of the past' (*RD* 124). His aesthetic cruelty is such that he can reject one of his daughters, 'the unlovely, graceless' (*RD* 34) Marigold, at the expense of the more pleasing Cora. When the barbarity of his artistic creed is made explicit, it is shown to be devoid of history and without blemishes of any kind. Those around him are either redeemed through their beauty or deemed to be redundant. On the level of dream, however, he thinks of his film-making as a 'surrealistic process' (*RD* 74) based on momentary epiphanies, such as the fleeting shot of 'The Hamburger Girl' (valued precisely because she has no past), which form the bedrock of his next movie. But he is never quite sure whether his characters are ghosts – something which he has dreamed up – or, in a repetition of Spark's personal theology, whether they are part of 'the age of the Holy Spirit, or as we used to say, Ghost' (*RD* 59). To this end, he thinks of himself as a 'character in one of God's dreams...They are real, frighteningly real. They bulge with flesh, they drip with blood' (*RD* 63–4).

Some reviewers of *Reality and Dreams* have argued that this reference to 'God's dreams' is reminiscent of the theatricality of God and Satan at the beginning of the book of Job or the Typing Ghost in *The Comforters*. There is certainly a strong sense of Spark's Job-driven theology at this point, which accepts that it is impossible to understand a God-given story of the world and yet acts as if there is 'a story of which we are all a part'. Others have interpreted this simultaneous rejection of and yearning for an all-explaining meta-narrative in secular terms as the key to understanding Spark's fiction.[6] What is clear is that the transformation of fragments of experience into a transcendent story, at the expense of one's own history and 'past ideas' (*RD* 75), is severely qualified in this work. Not unlike the figure of Margaret in *Symposium*, Marigold acts as a witch-like presence in the book, who disrupts the overweening certainties of Tom's imagistic and impressionistic film-making. By disappearing and playing dead, like so many of Spark's powerfully absent characters, Marigold forces Tom to explore the misplaced foundations of his impersonal artistry. Like Spark herself, who has moved from a too easy transfiguration of her past to its decisive inclusion in her fiction, Tom eventually brings his unruly daughter within the fragile sphere of art.

By ending her twentieth novel in 'the tract of no-man's-land between dreams and reality, reality and dreams' (*RD* 160), Spark has, to a large extent, come full circle. One remembers the 'No-Man's Sanatorium' inhabited by the hybrid Samuel Cramer in 'The Ballad of the Fanfarlo' (1952) or, even, the no-man's-land inhabited by the Mandelbaum Gate in Spark's heterodox novel of split identities and unplaceable individuals. The tension between the uncontrolled emotions unleashed by Marigold and Margaret and the need to order and aestheticize the world has been an abiding concern of many of Spark's personae, and culminates with Tom Richards. Spark is attracted to the spontaneous and unexplainable forces of nature – which are increasingly found at the heart of her beguiling artistry – while recognizing the necessity of containing such experiences within an ordered and sustained narrative. When she goes too far in one direction, and focuses on the originary chaos of her formative years, she reacts by moving towards a more coldly impersonal mode of fiction-making. In the end, the remarkable Muriel Spark has found some kind of comfort in the no-man's-land between the sufferings of reality and the etherized delights of a dream-like art.

Postscript:
The Facts of Blood

Muriel Spark's twenty-first novel *Aiding and Abetting* (2000) is in press at the same time as this book is nearing completion. It is probably not her last work of fiction as the eighty-two year old Spark, still waking at seven every morning to write, has begun another novel entitled *The Finishing School* which purportedly returns her to the familiar world of snobbery and social manners, a subject which she has always found ripe for satire.[1] *Aiding and Abetting*, however, is a fitting late work as it is an implicit summation of many of her fictional concerns. Much vaster in scope than her previous two novels, it encompasses Central Africa and the Scottish Highlands as well as London and Paris. The book's heroine, Dr Hildegard Wolf (also known as Beate Pappenheim), came from 'Bavaria, then Prague, Dresden, Avila, Marseilles, then London, and [is] now settled in Paris (*AA* 1). While Hildegard is in a long line of Sparkian cosmopolitan heroines, she is unusual in having a wholly other personal history. Born Beate Pappenheim on a pig farm in rural Nuremberg, she managed to escape extreme poverty by becoming a 'fake stigmatic' (*AA* 16) who tricked thousands of Catholics into sending her 'many millions of marks' (*AA* 16). After changing her identity she became Dr Hildegard Wolf, a celebrated psychiatrist practising in the centre of Paris.

The novel begins with the figure of Lord Lucan, wanted for bludgeoning his children's nanny to death in 1974, visiting Hildegard at her office so that he can recount his typical 'English story' (*AA* 1). While this is unusual in itself – the actual Lord Lucan has famously never been captured and is thought to have died some years ago – it is compounded by the bizarre fact that Hildegard already has a 'Lord Lucan' as a patient. As with Hildegard's dual self, the two Lord Lucans indicate the extent to which everything in *Aiding and Abetting* is doubled and redoubled. Spark's fiction has always been fascinated with doubles and, from her earliest work, the act of doubling is closely related to the act of writing. The double vision of Dougal Douglas or Douglas Dougal in *The Ballad of Peckham Rye* (1960) announces not only his spiritual role in Peckham (going beyond the pervading materialism) but his eventual vocation as a novelist. Jenny Gray and Sandy Stranger in *The Prime of Miss Jean Brodie* (1961) similarly listen to Miss Jean Brodie with sceptical 'double ears' (*PMJB* 72) which enables Sandy especially, a nascent author, to see beyond Brodie's mythomania. Such doubleness is both at the heart of Spark's fiction-making and is also a key element of her often ambiguous sense of virtue.

On one level, there is something strangely plausible in Lord Lucan seeking out Hildegard even though he knows her to be a bogus (albeit highly successful) psychiatrist. It turns out that they have a good deal in common although Spark is at pains to differentiate her two main characters. Lucan, after all, plans to blackmail Hildegard and is an avowed murderer and therefore occupies a completely distinct moral sphere from his would-be therapist. But both figures are fugitives from the law, who have been on the run for most of their lives, and both have been forced to assume alternative identities (Spark's Lucan undergoes plastic surgery). Beate Pappenheim's blood ritual, in particular, is dramatically related to Lucan's murder victim, Sandra Rivett, whose blood 'got everywhere. Pools of it' (*AA* 36). Beate, the holy stigmatic, who is also based on an actual person, imitated one of the five wounds of Christ by covering herself in menstrual blood so that it would seep through her bandaged hands, feet or sides. These spurious 'wounds' were a sign of her 'healing powers' (*AA* 23) which in a typical Sparkian paradox, actually helped her perform minor 'miracles' (*AA* 24). After the murder, Lucan also was 'so covered in blood' (*AA* 47) that bloodstains appeared on his clothes and letters sent immediately to friends. By the end of *Aiding and Abetting*, in fact, Lucan makes the blood-connection explicit between himself and Hildegard – 'we're both in this blood-business together, he seemed to say' (*AA* 123) –

although it is precisely these superficial similarities which are countered throughout the book.

Aiding and Abetting is literally dripping in blood which, as Hildegard notes, is absolutely everywhere: 'blood, once let loose, gets all over the place. It sticks, it flows, it garishly advertises itself or accumulates in thick dark puddles. Once it gets going, there is no stopping blood' (*AA* 121). To some extent this is a reprise of the plot of the novel which, in contrast to Spark's usual poetic economy, does not stop talking about the 'facts of blood' (*AA* 51). Lucan, it turns out, only eats smoked salmon and lamb chops which enables him to contrast his daily diet with the purifying 'Blood of the Lamb' (*AA* 42). This fundamental distinction between blood as bodily fluid or mere matter and the transfiguration of the blood of Christ clearly undercuts a too easy reduction of Hildegard and Lucan to mere 'blood-business'. More than any other novel since the 1970s, Spark in this work goes back to first principles and restates her Catholic orthodoxy with regard to a 'sacramental vision of the world' (*RA* 1) which enables the 'facts of blood' in the novel to inhabit both the physical and spiritual domains.

As always, however, such theological distinctions take an aesthetic as well as a moral form. Hildegard and Lucan both practice implicitly the dubious arts of fiction-making which gives weight to Frank Kermode's contention that Spark is a 'monologic' novelist whose characters 'all speak in some version of her voice'.[2] By doubling the possible accounts of the writer (one good, one bad), there is an explicit authorial investment in exactly the kind of story-telling which Spark approves of. Hildegard's unique method of therapy is, in these terms, a heady mixture of religious faith as well as the writerly arts. As a way of gradually inducing her patients to speak about themselves, the first three meetings with Hildegard consists of them listening passively to her talk about herself. Hers is a listening rather than a talking cure. While others have copied the 'Wolf method' (*AA* 2), Spark's narrator insists that 'the method alone did not suffice. Her personality was needed as well' (*AA* 2). Not unlike an ideal Sparkian novelist, Hildegard's force of personality is designed to encourage others to tell their stories. In perhaps a too easy synthesis, Hildegard's method of therapy is also given a God-like supremacy at the point when she advises a troubled priest to adopt her listening cure. As the priest puts it:

> 'She advised me not to try and pray. She advised me to shut up and listen. Read the gospel, she said. Jesus is praying to you for sympathy. You have to see his point of view, what he had to put up with. Listen, don't talk. Read the Bible. Take it in. God is talking, not you.' (*AA* 2–3)

Whereas Hildegard is the best possible model of the writer (combining her distinctive voice with the highest authority), Lord Lucan is deemed explicitly to be a bad novelist in both aesthetic and moral terms:

> What dream-like, immature culture was [Lucan] influenced by? For, surely, he had thought his plan to kill his wife was watertight. Whereas, even if the nanny had taken her night off, even if he had murdered the countess, the plot leaked at every seam as truly as did the blood-oozing mailbag into which the body of Sandra Rivett was packed. (*AA* 120)

The sensational conflation of metaphor and reality at the end of this statement – which brings together the leaky plot of an ill-thought out novel and a 'blood-oozing mailbag' – shows just how dangerous Spark's narrator regards an 'immature culture' to be. In these terms, Lucan is the last of her evil writers manqués, such as Lister in *Not to Disturb* (1971), who attempt to shape the world according to their own insane preoccupations: 'Lucan believed in destiny. By virtue of destiny he was an earl. His wife had been destined to die, according to his mad calculation... he "needed" his wife dead, and it was destiny' (*AA* 131). While Hildegard is open to a myriad of different voices, Lucan's 'sense of destiny obliterated the constant' (*AA* 132) and replaced it with a bad fiction.

To counter the rather predictable separation of Spark's two main characters, we are told that one of Lucan's many occupations since he murdered Sandra Rivett includes the priesthood and he has yet to throw off his 'theological look' (*AA* 53). The oft-repeated fact that Hildegard actually 'worked some miracles' (*AA* 53) also turns her into something of a white witch not unlike Marigold and Margaret in Spark's last two novels. This association is underlined by Spark's narrator, a little too heavy-handedly, when we are told that Hildegard's 'interest in voodoo, in blood cults and fraudulent mystifications was very genuine' (*AA* 142). As with so many of Spark's heroines, Hildegard is determinedly heterodox in her paganism as well as being overly cerebral – at one point replacing her lover with her 'clinical notes' (*AA* 112). What brings Lucan and Hildegard together, however, is their mutual fear of the past with Hildegard noting from the beginning that: 'I am being threatened...about some past life of mine, something in another world. It's upsetting me. Not rationally, of course. But I don't know quite what to do' (*AA* 18). Both are haunted by the 'memories of the past' (*AA* 51) and both have a 'bloody secret' (*AA* 44) which they attempt to expunge.

The radical rejection of the past takes a number of forms but indicates, above all, a peculiarly hedonistic regard for the present. One of the pleasures of reading *Aiding and Abetting* is its skilful use of the conventions of the detective novel where the past is routinely unravelled and accounted for. Lucan is investigated by Dr Joseph Murray, in his sixties, and Lacey Twickenham, in her thirties, who eventually forget about their potentially disabling obsession with Lucan and instead embark on a 'love affair, free and full of enterprise, without any mess or impediments' (*AA* 91). Their love-making, in other words, turns their detective work into mere game-playing. By the end of the book, they recount joyfully the many times in which they barely missed their prey. This story-line is related to Hildgard's lover Jean-Pierre who has a workshop which is 'like a junk heap of Europe' (*AA* 19) where bits of antiquity are transformed into fabulous contemporary pieces of wood and metal. Not unlike the ideal Sparkian artist, his consummate skill and craftsmanship literally redeems the waste of the past and turns it into something pleasurable. History, it seems, is either bunk or a threat with the present moment of beauty and laughter superseding an often grim set of antecedents.

By erasing their personal histories, both Lucan and Hildegard regard their new-found identities as a kind of performance. While Hildegard is at pains to distinguish between the real and false Lucan in moral terms – one is a murderer – she says of the impostor, Robert Walker, that 'after twenty-five years of playing the part of the missing Lord Lucan he surely is the part' (*AA* 48). After dying her hair blonde Hildegard hardly recognises her new guise, one of many which she assumes throughout the novel:

> Hildegard thought she saw in the large mirror over the mantelpiece another woman behind her. But on looking back, there was nobody. Of course, my blonde hair, Hildegard remembered. (*AA* 152)

Spark's sympathetic protagonists have long been characterized by their ability to see themselves from the outside as if they were a different person. Caroline Rose in *The Comforters* (1957), for instance, realised that to write a novel the 'narrative would never become coherent to her until she was at last outside it, and at the same time consummately inside it' (*C* 181). Being simultaneously both inside and outside her experience precisely defines Caroline as a novelist in Sparkian terms. At its best, this doubleness leads to a generosity of spirit and ingrained pluralism which in *Aiding and Abetting* challenges the biological determinism inherent in the 'facts of blood'. That is why Jean-Pierre defends Hildegard's spoof activities as a holy stigmatic with the following observation: 'I don't blame her for doing something constructive with her own blood. What else should a woman of imagination do with her menstrual blood?' (*AA* 158). Hildegard's imagination can transform her personal circumstances as well as the most mundane biological functions whereas Lucan, utterly devoid of imagination, fails to abolish the 'blood' and 'mess' (*AA* 163) which he had unleashed in 1974. In a crucial difference, Lucan's doubleness results not in a transfiguration of experience but in a baleful sense of himself as a 'dead man' (*AA* 15). For this reason Hildegard cites *The Comedy of Errors* and dismisses Lucan as '"a mere anatomy, a mountebank...a living-dead man"' (*AA* 124).

But these didactic distinctions are eventually undermined by the novel's ending. In a bid to avoid penury, both Lucans migrate to Kanzia, a fictitious country in Central Africa, to tutor the children of Chief Delihu Kanzia. The Chief argues that his many children will benefit from consuming one of the Lucans – as 'we become in some measure what we eat' (*AA* 180) – and, while preferring the innocent Walker, they mistakenly devour the actual Lord Lucan. This glorious parody of the transubstantiation results in Chief Delihu's children being turned in part into 'little Lord Lucans' (*AA* 181). Rather than a single act of sacramental redemption, such as washing in the blood of the lamb which makes everyone 'white' (*AA* 178), Spark ends with an extraordinarily charged moment of comic playfulness and plurality.

By the last chapter of *Aiding and Abetting* the 'facts of blood' are thrown into disarray with the tribe of Chief Kanzia, in a delightful instance of colonial mimicry, transformed bodily into members of the English aristocracy. Lucan's implacable sense of destiny is replaced by any number of possible racial destinations. The Roman Catholic consumption of the body of Christ is here related farcically to the sensitive issue of tribal cannibalism. But this is Spark's fiction at its most exciting where the reader has to work out the ambiguities of such risk-taking. On the one hand, the myriad of African Lord Lucans is a typical instance of Sparkian poetic justice (Lucan finally gets his comeuppance). Such game-playing also recalls the parodies of fundamental Catholic tenets which have been an aspect of Spark's writing since her African story 'Bang-Bang You're Dead' (1961) contained a child-like pastiche of the resurrection. But the association of cannibalism with either Catholic ritual or Africa is, to say the least, a combustible issue. *Aiding and Abetting* is thus both dangerously anarchic as well as haughtily moralistic.

The preoccupation with newly recreated identities which are able to transform the extremes of emotion – whether it be Lucan's murderous rage or Beate's miraculous transfigurations – relates *Aiding and Abetting* to Spark's work as a whole. Her twenty-first novel can, in this regard, be considered to be a key instance of her profound engagement with the narrative of conversion or what her authorial voice describes as 'people-within-people hitherto unknown' (*AA* 62). In his *The Book of God* (1988), Gabriel Josipovici has usefully placed the Pauline and Augustinian tradition of conversion at the beginning of the rise of the modern novel. According to this argument, the auto-biographical narratives of both St. Paul and St. Augustine demonstrate the need to 'talk in order to fix the flux of inner turmoil and objectify the crucial act of conversion'. They were the first, in other words, to stress the internal life of the spirit and the consequent meaninglessness of the external world:

> With this step Paul opens up a whole new world of inwardness, a world he himself explores and describes with passionate detail, and

which will always have room for fresh explorers, such as Augustine, Pascal and Rousseau. Yet the cost of this is high. Giving up the world of confusion, uncertainty and limited horizons for the apparent surer world of the spirit, he condemns himself to the sustaining vision of nothing other than the sheer power of the imagination and the constant reiteration of the drama of conversion.[3]

Elsewhere in *The Book of God* Josipovici argues that Spark's fiction, unlike the Pauline and Augustinian confessional tradition, 'turned its back on the probing of the inner life and accepted that the true springs of life are best tapped through dialogue and action'. But it is also true that Spark's fiction is a 'constant reiteration of the drama of conversion' and has a sustaining vision based principally on the 'power of the imagination' being able to transform an abiding sense of 'flux and inner turmoil.'[4]

Josipovici's stress on Pauline conversion as a way of inwardly redressing a world of confusion is worth noting in relation to Spark's heroine, Dr Hildegard Wolf. It is not a coincidence, in this regard, that Beate Pappenheim, Hildegard's alter ego, is quite literally a beatification of one of the most famous patients in the history of psychoanalysis, Bertha Pappenheim. Better known as 'Anna O.', Bertha Pappenheim appears in Joseph Breuer's and Sigmund Freud's *Studies in Hysteria* (1895) and subsequently became the first social worker in Frankfurt-am-Main and founder of the German-Jewish feminist movement.[5] As Beate is born in a pig farm in rural Nuremberg, she could not be further removed from the biography of Bertha Pappenheim. At the same time, Beate and Bertha are brought together in relation to the scientific pretensions of psychoanalysis which, not unlike religious conversion, is meant to be able to cure the diseased and unstable mind. But, as Josipovici shows, Spark's fiction above all demonstrates the impossibility of such a cure as the certainties of the inner life are merely illusory and have to be reimagined constantly.

Much of Spark's later fiction concerns the overwhelming ascendancy of dream-like states which is perhaps why the protagonist of her last novel *Reality and Dreams* (1996) regards himself as a 'character in one of God's dreams...They are real, frighteningly real. They bulge with flesh, they drip with blood' (*RD* 63–5). As in *Aiding and Abetting*, blood is only minimally a question of biology and is instead associated with the excesses of unreal emotions and (as blood seeps everywhere) with the uneasy relation between the inner and outer self or dreams and reality. Many of her books are haunted by the enduring presence of ghosts, phantoms and spirits of all kinds not unlike the fissured body in *Territorial Rights* (1979). As in *The Mandelbaum Gate*, her characters often 'believe with their blood' (*MG* 17) which can result either in an empty fanaticism or a more creative supernaturalism. Her recent use of the epigraph from Lucian's *Symposium* – 'the party was finally broken up by the shedding of blood' (*S* 5) – also enacts a characteristic tension between a civilized decorum and the uncontrollable passions ready to be unleashed in the most unexpected ways.

Spark's novels in general refuse to be taken in by the easy oppositions which define the Pauline conversionist narrative – 'Law/Grace, Works/Faith, Old Man/New Man, Jew/Christian, blindness/sight' – or, in more modern terms, the language of reason and madness.[6] Beate Pappenheim or Hildegard Wolf is both a Gentile Jewess and a doctor/patient, the last of many such hybrid figures, and is therefore a subtle means of replacing a conversionist orthodoxy with a unique perspective beyond such received banalities. It is in this singular context that Hildegard attempts to identify a 'morality devoid of ethics or civil law' (*AA* 34) and why Joseph Murray argues that it is 'possible...for a man to be a holy person and a glib liar at the same time' (*AA* 89). Spark's authorial voice understands only too well the dangers of creating a wholly redeemed self based on the capricious artistry of the writer. Because of this acute awareness she cites part of Shakespeare's Sonnet 111 which sounds awfully like an aesthetic credo:

> ...My nature is subdued
> To what it works in, like the dyer's hand.

> (*AA* 48)

Here we have not just a transcendence of predetermined blood-lines (one's 'nature') but a strong sense of the necessary artifice which distinguishes so many of Spark's sympathetic protagonists. While the aptly named Hildegard *Wolf* is described as 'an animal trying to put that man [Walker] off the scent' (*AA* 18), she is also a determinedly self-made creation. This unresolved tension between the demands of life and of art is perfectly expressed in the phrase 'dyer's hand' which sums up the impossible quest of the writer to subdue nature. Hildegard's ability to contain so many possible realities and to overcome her extreme poverty by the sheer force of her imagination resonates throughout Spark's fiction. Such is the self-confidence in the capacity of art to redeem the most inauspicious of origins. But Spark's greatness resides in the fact that her fiction demonstrates that the 'dyer's hand' can itself be covered in blood and when art is abused - as in the case of Lord Lucan and other mythomaniac figures of evil - it can be implicated in the horror as well as the beauty of the modern world.

Notes

CHAPTER 1.   LIFE-STORIES: REDEEMING THE PAST

1   Frank Kermode, 'A Turn of Events', *London Review of Books*, 14 November 1996, 23–4.
2   Bent Nordhjem, *What Fiction Means*, PDE (Publications of the Department of English, University of Copenhagen), vol. 15 (1987), p. 140, cited in Martin McQuillan (ed.), *Theorising Muriel Spark: Gender, Psychoanalysis, Deconstruction* (London: Macmillan, 2001).
3   Key figures who regard Spark in the highest possible terms include Malcolm Bradbury, Graham Greene, Gabriel Josipovici, Frank Kermode, David Lodge, John Updike and Evelyn Waugh. It is curious that women critics have been somewhat less effusive.
4   Alan Bold, *Muriel Spark* (London: Methuen, 1986), 11.
5   Patrick Parrinder, 'Muriel Spark and her Critics', *Critical Quarterly*, 25 (Summer 1983), 26.
6   Peter Kemp, *Muriel Spark: Novelists and Their World* (London: Paul Elek, 1974), 158.
7   Jennifer Lynn Randisi, *On Her Way Rejoicing: The Fiction of Muriel Spark* (Washington DC: The Catholic University of America Press, 1991), chapter 4.
8   Gauri Viswanathan, *Outside the Fold: Conversion, Modernity, and Belief* (New Jersey: Princeton University Press, 1998), p. xvii and chapter 1.
9   I am grateful to Laura Marcus for this argument.
10   Ruth Whittaker, *The Faith and Fiction of Muriel Spark* (London and Basingstoke: Macmillan, 1982), 37, and Randisi, *On Her Way Rejoicing*, for this argument *ad nauseam*.
11   Karl Malkoff, *Muriel Spark* (New York: Columbia University Press, 1968), 5.
12   Malcolm Bradbury, 'Muriel Spark's Fingernails', in *No, Not Bloomsbury* (London: Arena, 1987), 271.
13   Michael André Bernstein, *Foregone Conclusions: Against Apocalyptic*

History (Berkeley: University of California Press, 1994).

14   Quoted in Bold, *Muriel Spark*, 26.

15   Muriel Spark, 'The Poet in Mr. Eliot's Ideal State', *Outposts*, vol. 14 (Summer 1949), 26–8. While Spark's 'My Conversion' (1961) is referred to extensively in many previous critical studies of her fiction, it has recently been repudiated by Spark herself. For an annotated version of the essay, in a bid to expose its inaccuracies, see the Muriel Spark Manuscript collection in the University of Tulsa, McFarlin Library, item 53:3.

16   Geordie Greig, 'The Dame's fortunes', *Sunday Times*, 22 September 1995, 8–9.

CHAPTER 2.   HALF-WORLDS: WRITING AGAINST CONVERSION

1   Patricia Waugh, *Metafiction: The Theory and Practice of Self-Conscious Fiction* (London: Methuen, 1984), 74.

2   Bernard Harrison, 'Muriel Spark and Jane Austen', in Gabriel Josipovici (ed.), *The Modern English Novel: the Reader, the Writer and the Work* (London: Open Books, 1976), 249–50.

3   Alan Bold, *Muriel Spark* (London: Methuen, 1986), 36.

4   Peter Kemp, *Muriel Spark: Novelists and Their World* (London: Paul Elek, 1974), 18.

5   Jennifer Lynn Randisi, *On Her Way Rejoicing: The Fiction of Muriel Spark* (Washington DC: The Catholic University of America Press, 1991), chapter 4.

6   For many of these traditional associations see Gillian Beer, 'The Island and the Aeroplane: the Case of Virginia Woolf', in Homi Bhabha (ed.), *Nation and Narration* (London: Routledge, 1990), chapter 15.

CHAPTER 3.   BEYOND ORTHODOXY: DEATH, DEMONS AND SINGULARITY

1   Patrick Parrinder, 'Muriel Spark and her Critics', *Critical Quarterly*, 25 (Summer 1983), 25.

2   Peter Kemp, *Muriel Spark: Novelists and Their World* (London: Paul Elek, 1974), 42.

3   Ibid., 43.

4   Patrick Parrinder, 'Muriel Spark and her Critics', *Critical Quarterly*, 25 (Summer 1983), for this argument.

5   Karl Malkoff, *Muriel Spark* (New York: Columbia University Press, 1968), 24.
6   Alan Bold, *Muriel Spark* (London: Methuen, 1986), 58–62.

CHAPTER 4.   TRANSFIGURATIONS: EDINBURGH, LONDON, JERUSALEM

1   David Lodge, *The Novelist at the Crossroads* (London: Routledge, 1971), 135.
2   Bernard Harrison, 'Muriel Spark and Jane Austen', in Gabriel Josipovici (ed.), *The Modern English Novel: the Reader, the Writer and the Work* (London: Open Books, 1976), 237.
3   Velma Bourgeois Richmond, *Muriel Spark* (New York: Frederick Ungar, 1984), 26.
4   Norman Page, *Muriel Spark* (London and Basingstoke: Macmillan, 1990), 48, for this essentially false etymology.
5   Ibid., 48–50.
6   Ruth Whittaker, *The Faith and Fiction of Muriel Spark* (London and Basingstoke: Macmillan, 1982), 78.
7   Both interviews are quoted in Whittaker, *The Faith and Fiction of Muriel Spark*, 79.
8   Jacqueline Rose, *States of Fantasy* (Oxford: Oxford University Press, 1996), 68–70.
9   Gabriel Josipovici, 'An evil eye overlooking the jet set', *Independent*, 22 September 1990, 29.
10   Hannah Arendt, *Eichmann in Jerusalem: A Report on the Banality of Evil* (Harmondsworth: Penguin Books, 1977).

CHAPTER 5.   MACHINE-MADE PARABLES: FROM SATIRE TO ABSURDITY

1   Angus Wilson, 'Journey to Jerusalem', *Observer*, 17 October 1965, 28.
2   *Guardian*, 30 September 1970, 8.
3   Ruth Whittaker, *The Faith and Fiction of Muriel Spark* (London and Basingstoke: Macmillan, 1982), 115–16.
4   Quoted in Gavin Wallace and Randall Stevenson (eds.), *The Scottish Novel Since the Seventies* (Edinburgh: Edinburgh University Press, 1993), 43–4.
5   Jennifer Lynn Randisi, *On Her Way Rejoicing: The Fiction of Muriel Spark* (Washington DC: The Catholic University of America Press, 1991), 27.

6   Malcolm Bradbury, 'Muriel Spark's Fingernails', in *No, Not Bloomsbury* (London: Arena, 1987), 273.
7   Douglas Gifford and Dorothy McMillan (eds.), *A History of Scottish Women's Writing* (Edinburgh: Edinburgh University Press, 1997), 522.
8   Alan Bold, *Muriel Spark* (London: Methuen, 1986), 95.

CHAPTER 6.   INTERNATIONAL MESSES: BETWEEN LIFE AND ART

1   Velma Bourgeois Richmond, *Muriel Spark* (New York: Frederick Ungar, 1984), 124.
2   Victoria Glendinning, 'Talk with Muriel Spark', *New York Times Book Review*, 20 May 1979, 47–8.
3   Alan Bold, *Muriel Spark* (London: Methuen, 1986), 98–9.
4   Ruth Whittaker, *The Faith and Fiction of Muriel Spark* (London and Basingstoke: Macmillan, 1982), 80, quotes examples of this scepticism.
5   Gavin Wallace and Randall Stevenson (eds.), *The Scottish Novel Since the Seventies* (Edinburgh: Edinburgh University Press, 1993), 47.
6   This subtitle seems only to have been used in the Penguin 1978 edition and has subsequently been discarded.
7   Bold, *Muriel Spark*, 24.
8   Marcel Proust, *In Search of Lost Time*, vol. 1 (London: Chatto & Windus, 1992), 54.
9   Michael Wood, 'Endangered Species', *New York Review of Books* (11 November 1970), 30.
10 Whittaker, *The Faith and Fiction of Muriel Spark*, 84.
11 Joseph Hynes, *The Art of the Real: Muriel Spark's Novels* (London and Toronto: Associated University Presses, 1988), 127.
12 Gabriel Josipovici, *Text and Voice: Essays 1981–1991* (Manchester: Carcanet, 1992), 237–8.
13 Patrick Parrinder, 'Muriel Spark and her Critics', *Critical Quarterly*, 25 (Summer 1983), 30.

CHAPTER 7.   HAUNTINGS: THE RETURN OF THE REPRESSED

1   John Updike, 'Fresh from the Forties', *New Yorker*, June 1981, 148–50.
2   Norman Page, *Muriel Spark* (London and Basingstoke: Macmillan, 1990), 102–3.

3   Alan Bold (ed.), *Muriel Spark: An Odd Capacity for Vision* (London and New Jersey: Vision & Barnes & Noble, 1984), 29.

4   Ibid.

5   Page, *Muriel Spark*, 104.

6   Laura Marcus, *Auto/biographical Discourses: Criticism, Theory, Practice* (Manchester: Manchester University Press, 1994), 7.

7   Aryeh Maidenbaum and Stephen A. Martin (eds.), *Lingering Shadows: Jungians, Freudians and Anti-Semitism* (Boston and London: Shambhala, 1991), 10–11, 83–6.

8   Harold Fisch, *A Remembered Future: A Study in Literary Mythology* (Bloomington: Indiana University Press, 1984), 164–5.

9   Gabriel Josipovici, 'On the Side of Job', *Times Literary Supplement*, 7 September, 1984, 989.

10   Ibid., and Frank Kermode, 'Old Testament Capers', *London Review of Books*, 20 September–3 October 1984, 10–11.

11   Peter Kemp, 'Loitering with intent in literary London', *Sunday Times*, 20 March 1988, 5.

12   Susannah Clapp, 'Pisseurs', *London Review of Books*, 2 June 1988, 16–17.

CHAPTER 8.   CONTINUITIES AND DISCONTINUITIES

1   Velma Bourgeois Richmond, *Muriel Spark* (New York: Frederick Ungar, 1984), 178 and Ruth Whittaker, *The Faith and Fiction of Muriel Spark* (London and Basingstoke: Macmillan, 1982), 150–1, for typical accounts of Spark in these terms. Alan Bold, *Muriel Spark* (London: Methuen, 1986), 119, for an interesting counter-reading.

2   Bold, *Muriel Spark*, 53.

3   Gabriel Josipovici, 'An evil eye overlooking the jet set', *Independent*, 22 September 1990, 29.

4   Emmanuel Levinas, *Autrement qu'être ou au delà de l'essence* (The Hague: Martinus Nijhoff, 1978).

5   Patrick Parrinder, 'Muriel Spark and her Critics', *Critical Quarterly*, 25 (Summer 1983), 26.

6   Antonia Byatt, 'The dreams of God', *Sunday Times*, 29 September 1996, 13, Patricia Waugh, *Metafiction: The Theory and Practice of Self-Conscious Fiction* (London: Methuen, 1984), 121–2, and Gabriel Josipovici, *The Book of God* (New Haven and London: Yale University Press, 1988), 289–90.

POSTSCRIPT: THE FACTS OF BLOOD

1   Emma Brockes, 'The Genteel Assassin' *The Guardian: Saturday Review* (May 27, 2000), 6–7.
2   Frank Kermode, 'Old Testament Capers', *London Review of Books* (20 September–3 October, 1984), 10–11.
3   Gabriel Josipovici, *The Book of God* (New Haven and London: Yale University Press, 1988), 251–53.
4   Ibid. 252. For a recent account of these issues from an uncritical perspective see Joseph Pearce, *Literary Converts: Spiritual Inspiration in an Age of Unbelief* (London: HarperCollins, 1999), chapter 23.
5   Daniel Boyarin, *Unheroic Conduct: The Rise of Heterosexuality and the Invention of the Jewish Man* (Berkeley: University of California Press, 1997), 28–9, 180–85 and chapter 8.
6   Josipovici, *The Book of God*, 241.

Select Bibliography

WORKS BY MURIEL SPARK

Novels

The Comforters (London: Macmillan, 1957).
Robinson (London: Macmillan, 1958).
Memento Mori (London: Macmillan, 1959).
The Ballad of Peckham Rye (London: Macmillan, 1960).
The Bachelors (London: Macmillan, 1960).
The Prime of Miss Jean Brodie (London: Macmillan, 1961).
The Girls of Slender Means (London: Macmillan, 1963).
The Mandelbaum Gate (London: Macmillan, 1965).
The Public Image (London: Macmillan, 1968).
The Driver's Seat (London: Macmillan, 1970).
Not to Disturb (London: Macmillan, 1971).
The Hothouse by the East River (London: Macmillan, 1973).
The Abbess of Crewe (London: Macmillan, 1974).
The Takeover (London: Macmillan, 1976).
Territorial Rights (London: Macmillan, 1979).
Loitering with Intent (London: The Bodley Head, 1981).
The Only Problem (London: The Bodley Head, 1984).
A Far Cry from Kensington (London: Constable, 1988).
Symposium (London: Constable, 1990).
Reality and Dreams (London: Constable, 1996).
Aiding and Abetting (London: Viking, 2000).

Short Stories

The Go-Away Bird and Other Stories (London: Macmillan, 1958).
Voices at Play (London: Macmillan, 1961).
Bang Bang You're Dead and Other Stories (St Albans: Granada, 1982).
The Collected Stories of Muriel Spark (Harmondsworth: Penguin Books,

142

1994).

Open to the Public: New and Collected Stories (New York: New Directions, 1997).

The Young Man who Discovered the Secret of Life and Other Stories (London: Travelman Publishing, 1999).

Non-Fiction

'The Poet in Mr Eliot's Ideal State', *Outposts*, 14 (Summer 1949).

'The Dramatic Works of T. S. Eliot', *Women's Review*, 5 (1949).

Tribute to Wordsworth: A Miscellany of Opinion for the Centenary of the Poet's Death, edited with Derek Stanford (London: Wingate, 1950).

Child of Light: A Reassessment of Mary Wolstonecraft Shelley (Hadleigh: Tower Bridge Publications, 1951).

A Selection of Poems by Emily Brontë (London: Grey Walls Press, 1952).

The Fanfarlo and Other Verse (Aldington, Kent: The Hand & Flower Press, 1952).

The Brontë Letters (London: Peter Nevill, 1953).

John Masefield (London: Peter Nevill, 1953).

Emily Brontë: Her Life and Work, edited with Derek Stanford (London: Peter Owen, 1953).

My Best Mary: Selected Letters of Mary Shelley, edited with Derek Stanford (London: Wingate, 1953).

'The Religion of an Agnostic: A Sacramental View of the World of Marcel Proust', *Church of England Newspaper*, 27 November, 1953.

'The Mystery of Job's Suffering', *Church of England Newspaper*, 15 April, 1955.

Letters of John Henry Newman, edited with Derek Stanford (London: Peter Owen, 1957).

'How I Became a Novelist', *John O'London's Weekly*, 1 December 1960.

'My Conversion', *The Twentieth Century* (Autumn, 1961).

Doctors of Philosophy (London: Macmillan, 1963).

Collected Poems 1 (London: Macmillan, 1967).

'What Images Return', in Karl Miller (ed.), *Memoirs of a Modern Scotland* (London: Faber & Faber, 1970).

'The Desegregation of Art', *Proceedings of the American Academy of Arts and Letters* (New York: The Blashfield Foundation, 1971).

Going up to Sotheby's and Other Poems (St Albans: Granada, 1982).

CRITICAL STUDIES

Bernstein, Michael André, *Foregone Conclusions: Against Apocalyptic History* (Berkeley: University of California Press, 1994). An excellent anti-determinist argument in relation to modern fiction.

Bold, Alan (ed.), *Muriel Spark: An Odd Capacity for Vision* (London: Vision Press, Ltd., 1984). Quirky and occasionally suggestive.

—— *Muriel Spark* (London: Methuen, 1986). A poet's eye view of Spark.

Bradbury, Malcolm (ed.), *The Novel Today: Contemporary Writers on Modern Fiction* (London: Fontana, 1977). Contains the essential 1963 interview between Spark and Frank Kermode.

—— *No, Not Bloomsbury* (London: Arena, 1987). Contains 'Muriel Spark's Fingernails'.

Gifford, Douglas and Dorothy McMillan (eds.), *A History of Scottish Women's Writing* (Edinburgh: Edinburgh University Press, 1997). Contains 'The Remarkable Fictions of Muriel Spark'.

Hynes, Joseph, *The Art of the Real: Muriel Spark's Novels* (London and Toronto: Associated University Presses, 1988). Largely unreadable, with some interesting ideas.

Josipovici, Gabriel (ed.), *The Modern English Novel: the Reader, the Writer and the Work* (London: Open Books, 1976). Contains the invaluable 'Muriel Spark and Jane Austen'.

—— *The Book of God* (New Haven and London: Yale University Press, 1988). Interesting readings of *The Only Problem*.

—— *Text and Voice: Essays 1981–1991* (Manchester: Carcanet, 1992). References to Spark and the modernist tradition.

Kemp, Peter, *Muriel Spark: Novelists and Their World* (London: Paul Elek, 1974). Some good individual readings of Spark's books.

Kermode, Frank, *The Sense of an Ending* (Oxford: Oxford University Press, 1966). Contains some influential readings of Spark.

—— *Modern Essays* (London: Fontana, 1971). Has an important chapter on Spark.

Lodge, David, *The Novelist at the Crossroads* (London: Routledge, 1971). Contains 'The Uses and Abuses of Omniscience: Method and Meaning in Muriel Spark's *The Prime of Miss Jean Brodie*'.

Malkoff, Karl, *Muriel Spark* (New York: Columbia University Press, 1968). The best early study of Spark.

McQuillan, Martin (ed.), *Theorising Muriel Spark: Gender, Psychoanalysis, Deconstruction* (London: Macmillan, 2001). The first sustained attempt to engage with Spark's work in a theoretically sophisticated manner.

Page, Norman, *Muriel Spark* (London: Macmillan, 1990). Largely a summary of secondary sources.

Parrinder, Patrick, 'Muriel Spark and her Critics', *Critical Quarterly*, 25 (Summer 1983), 23–31. Still useful and suggestive.

Randisi, Jennifer Lynn, *On Her Way Rejoicing: The Fiction of Muriel Spark* (Washington DC: The Catholic University of America Press, 1991).

Treats Spark merely as a Catholic writer.

Richmond, Velma Bourgeois, *Muriel Spark* (New York: Frederick Ungar, 1984). Descriptive with some useful information.

Rose, Jacqueline, *States of Fantasy* (Oxford: Oxford University Press, 1996). Has an interesting chapter on Spark's *The Mandelbaum Gate*.

Wallace, Gavin, and Randall Stevenson (eds.), *The Scottish Novel Since the Seventies* (Edinburgh: Edinburgh University Press, 1993). Contains 'The Deliberate Cunning of Muriel Spark'.

Waugh, Patricia, *Metafiction: The Theory and Practice of Self-Conscious Fiction* (London: Methuen, 1984). Contains some interesting readings of Spark.

Whittaker, Ruth, *The Faith and Fiction of Muriel Spark* (London and Basingstoke: Macmillan, 1982). Still influential but limited in its approach.

Index

Africa, 4–5
avant-garde movements,
    influence on Spark, 9, 35, 71

Baudelaire, Charles, 12

Cellini, Benvenuto, 103, 108
Coleridge, Samuel Taylor, 61
conversion, 6, 11, 13, 14, 20–5
    passim, 63, 72, 74, 101–2, 108,
    110, 132–3

Defoe, Daniel, 33, 35

Edinburgh, 15, 53, 55, 58
Eliot, T. S., 16, 81, 123–4

Ford, Ford Madox, 9

Golding, William, 33
Greene, Graham, 2, 9

Hogg, James, 45
Hopkins, Gerard Manley, 61

Jerusalem, 53, 64
Jewishness, 16–19, 26–7, 63–4, 66
Job, book of, 108–14 *passim*
Joyce, James, 13, 17
Jung, Carl Gustav, 110

Levinas, Emmanuel, 122
London, 53

Masefield, John, 3

Newman, John Henry, 8, 103, 108

Pappenheim, Bertha, 133
Proust, Marcel, 17, 25–6, 31, 50,
    95, 96

Robbe-Grillet, Alain, 71

Scottishness, 15, 16
Spark, Muriel
    The Abbess of Crewe (1974), 84,
        88–92, 96, 100, 101, 118
    Aiding and Abetting (2000),
        126–35
    'Another Pair of Hands'
        (1985), 7
    The Bachelors (1960), 47–50, 53,
        64, 71, 94, 95, 96
    'The Ballad of the Fanfarlo'
        (1952), 11, 46, 125
    The Ballad of Peckham Rye
        (1960), 7, 13, 16, 43–7, 50,
        52, 58, 77, 119, 127
    'Bang-Bang You're Dead'
        (1961), 5, 13, 132
    'The Black Madonna' (1958),
        19, 116
    'Come Along Marjorie' (1958),
        10–11
    The Comforters (1957), 1, 2, 9,
        21–35 *passim*, 47, 50, 63, 64,